Rainbow in the Word

Rainbow in the Word

LGBTQ Christians' Biblical Memoirs

Edited by

ELLIN STERNE JIMMERSON

Foreword by
VIKI MATSON

WIPF & STOCK · Eugene, Oregon

RAINBOW IN THE WORD
LGBTQ Christians' Biblical Memoirs

Wipf & Stock
An Imprint of Wipf and Stock Publishers
199 W. 8th Ave., Suite 3
Eugene, OR 97401

www.wipfandstock.com

PAPERBACK ISBN: 978-1-5326-3208-2
HARDCOVER ISBN: 978-1-5326-3210-5
EBOOK ISBN: 978-1-5326-3209-9

Manufactured in the U.S.A.   JULY 11, 2017

To my mother, Elinor Crawford Sterne,
and to the memory of my father, Edwin Leggett Sterne,
who taught me that Jesus is about freedom.

So if anyone is in Christ, there is a new creation:
everything old has passed away;
see, everything has become new!

—2 Cor 5:17

Contents

CONTENTS

Foreword

In my city of Nashville there is a downtown intersection about which most people don't give another thought. Down by the river, Church Street intersects Gay Street with "Church" pointing one way and "Gay" pointing the other. This has become, for me, a metaphor of the struggle that queer folk often have with all things religious.

As LGBTQ folks come of age, there are many authorities, institutions, and moral codes to be navigated. It requires a formidable kind of soul-searching and wrestling. Essential to this process are honesty with oneself and others, an intellectual curiosity and willingness to rethink long-held assumptions, deep respect for the mystery of God, and courage to claim one's own life. It is no wonder then that among the wisest, most integrated, and genuine people I know are a fair number of LGBTQ folk. The furnace of struggle has been a refining one.

Rainbow in the Word: LGBTQ Christians' Biblical Memoirs includes the marks and memories of this struggle, particularly as the struggle involves the Bible. Some writers reflect on a particular text, wondering if there are ways to understand it that reveal a liberating rather than a punishing God. Others identify with a particular character in the Bible, diving deeply into their story to unearth what might be hidden or neglected. Some speak of the ways they have been wounded by Scripture, while others speak of being freed by it. Additionally, within these pages you will find genres as disparate as those contained within the Bible itself: narrative, confession, poetry, biography, and calls to action.

Each of us is a theologian to the extent that we find ourselves pondering big questions that affect our lives. What is the nature of God? What might it mean to be created in God's image? Is my difference (queerness) a mistake or a blessing? How are we to think of sin? How are we to regard the gift of sexuality? What makes the Bible authoritative for people of faith?

These questions take on particular importance for queer folk because so often the tenets of the faith have been used to hurt, shame, or destroy individual souls. Freeing oneself from the effects of this harm can take a lifetime because it has to do with rethinking foundational beliefs we were taught since we were children. It is soul-defining work, and we would do well to find others to go this hard way with us.

At its core, the Bible is a book about liberation. It chronicles a whole people as they traverse out of slavery in the land of Egypt and into the Promised Land where they are free. It contains the writings and speeches of prophets who railed against the status quo, calling at every turn for more fairness and justice—God's justice. And in the New Testament, of course, we encounter the person of Jesus who reached out to those on the margins, who challenged the false piety of the religious leaders, and who, with every word he spoke, envisioned a different kind of world marked by love, hospitality, and humility.

Religious leaders would be wise to reflect on the writings of this book. Perhaps then, one fine day, the signs of "church" and "gay" need not point in opposite directions. May it be so.

Viki Matson
Vanderbilt University Divinity School
Nashville, Tennessee

Preface

R *ainbow in the Word: LGBTQ Christians' Biblical Memoirs* began when one of the contributors, Kenny Pierce, posted a question on Facebook which had theological, anthropological, and biblical implications. Referencing both the book of Esther and his own experience as a gay Christian, he wondered whether God had put lesbians, gay men, bisexuals, transgender, and queer (LGBTQ) people on earth to bring healing to our broken world. I was so taken by his question and his post that I found myself absorbed by questions of my own which arose out of them. How have other LGBTQ Christians processed their experiences using the Bible as a filter? Do LGBTQ Christians have anything special to offer biblical interpretation? What do LGBTQ Christians bring to the table for other LGBTQ Christians struggling with issues of their own sexuality, particularly as they run into stumbling blocks, whether real or perceived, of the Bible, the church, and Christian cultures? What do LGBTQ Christians bring to the table for those of us, like me, who are straight Christians?

Acting somewhat impulsively, I sent out a call for submissions for an anthology, wondering whether there were enough LGBTQ Christians who think critically about the Bible, who have interesting personal stories they bounce off the Bible, and who write well. As this volume shows, the answer to my question is a resounding "yes!" Without any doubt there are far more LGBTQ

Christians out there who have their own stories to tell, their own biblical interpretations to offer, their own words of counsel and comfort. There surely will be more volumes like this for which we all will be the richer.

Ellin Sterne Jimmerson

Acknowledgments

F ew people can do anything of worth without encouragement. No woman ever had a greater cheerleader than I do in my husband, Al Jimmerson. He brings me coffee in the morning, pays my bills, and offers me free legal advice. He is a keeper. When other people had problems with me officiating at the first same-sex wedding in Madison County, Alabama, my daughter, Whitney Detwiler, let it be known she was proud of me. It is not for nothing I have always called her my "treasure person" because, as the Bible says, "where your treasure is, there your heart will be also" (Matt 6:21). I owe a debt of gratitude to my friends, Jeff Hood, a queer Christian, and Randy Culbreth, a gay Christian, who have been encouraging me for a long time to write a book. Finally, I owe an enormous debt to the contributors to this volume for trusting me with your stories and your points of view. It cannot be easy to turn sensitive pieces of yourself over to someone you do not know. Thank you all for your trust.

Ellin Sterne Jimmerson

Introduction

There may be no Christians who have been more maligned by their own church and fellow Christians over a longer period of time than lesbians, gay men, bisexual, transgender, genderqueer, and other non-heterosexual, non-gender conforming, or non-sexually normative people. It seems appropriate to begin with a word or two about language—words and acronyms. You will see one of the acronyms for some of the people described above—LGBTQ—throughout this book. This stands for lesbians, gay men, bisexual, transgender, and, variously, questioning or queer people. However, the acronym does not reflect everyone who is not both cisgender (a person whose outward body appearance conforms to society's expectations of them as far as gender is concerned) and heterosexual (a person who is sexually attracted only to people at the opposite end of the gender spectrum). There are other acronyms which some prefer—LGBTQI (for "inquiring"), LGBTQIA (for "ally" or straight people like me), and GLBT, among others. For the sake of simplicity only, I have decided to use LGBTQ throughout. It is a term which, to some degree because of the "Q," has a good bit of flexibility built into it.

You also will encounter the word "queer" throughout this book. Queer is a word used a slur throughout the past century at least. For some, especially for those over the age of fifty or so, it continues to function not only as a slur but as a trigger word that opens old wounds. For others, especially younger LGBTQ people, it is a word that has been embraced and rehabilitated. For them, it is a kind of umbrella term embracing lesbian, gay, bisexual, transgender, genderqueer, and anyone who is not cisgender and heterosexual. Partly, the rehabilitation of the word "queer" reflects current thinking on gender and sexuality that is similar to current thinking about race—each is a powerful social construct which exists along a sort of sliding scale. This means that gender and sexual categories are, as categories, social inventions. Just as it might be difficult to know whether a girl with skin the color of café au lait and green eyes is genetically African, Asian, or European, it is often difficult to determine by looking at someone whether they are gay or straight, male or female, gay and straight, male and female, or are somewhere else along the gender and sexuality scale.

Nonetheless, gender and sexuality are social constructs which, like the construct of race, has brutalizing power. That it is a construct has not stopped Christians, among others, from attempting to place people into rigid categories insisting that all humanity naturally is divided into straight male or straight female. It has not stopped far too many Christians from concluding that although café au lait skin color or green eyes is not a choice, gender and sexuality are. It has not stopped them from assigning moral superiority to heterosexual males and females who present unambiguously as heterosexual males and females and moral inferiority to everyone else.

Most significantly for purposes of this book, it has not stopped Christians and the church generally from using the Bible to abuse LGBTQ people. Using the Bible to abuse them—or anyone else—is a serious problem. It is a serious indictment of Christians and the church. It is especially troubling since Christians and the church are supposed to bring Good News to everyone. Using the Bible to abuse people, however, is not Good News for them—it is Bad News. It is Bad News for people who are told over and over and over, supposedly by God in God's Word, that they are fundamentally flawed, that they are an abomination, a pervert, a corruption.

In the essays that follow, you will encounter important by-products of this kind of abuse—shame and fear. Guilt, the emotion sometimes confused with shame, is a good and necessary emotion that helps us understand that something we did was wrong. Shame, by contrast, is the terrible sense that one is inherently wrong. The sense of shame so many LGBTQ people live with is made even worse by being told over and over, with Bible verses at the ready to clinch the point, that they are making a choice. They hear over and over that if they would make the right choice—to stop being gay—they could get right not only with their families and the church but with God.

There are roughly seven passages in the Bible which most often are used to beat up gays spiritually, to instill shame in them, and to create the deadly disease of homophobia which leads to their social isolation, family abandonment, murder, suicide, attempts to escape the pain with alcohol and drugs, and even legislation against them with penalties including death. Known as the "major clobber verses," they are Gen 19, Lev 18:22 and 20:13, Rom 1:26–27, 1 Cor 6:9–10, 1 Tim 1:9–10, and Jude 1:7. You will find explicit references to the clobber passages in some of the entries, but they hover in the background of many if not all of the other entries.

Whether these clobber verses actually condemn homosexuality is not the issue. Some Bible scholars conclude they do; others conclude they do not. The issue is that somewhere between seven and twenty isolated texts are being used against people we straight Christians love to call our brothers and sisters in horrifying and even criminal ways. As a consequence, LGBTQ Christians live not only with shame but in fear. They live in fear of being found out. They live in fear of being excluded or abandoned. They live in fear of taking the next step and coming out or making the transition from male to female, female to male. The systematic generation of shame and fear on the part of Christians and our church by using the Bible is a problem to say the least. It is a problem for gays, it is a problem for straights, it is a problem for the church, and it is a problem for God.

While it is difficult to make claims for other people, these essays have shown me that many LGBTQ Christians are clinging to the Bible. This, in itself, is remarkable and worthy of note. They cling to it for a way out, not of their queerness, but for a way out of shame and its destructiveness. They cling to it because they are tired of being afraid. They cling to it because in it they find hope—the profound sense that the future can be different from and better than the present. They believe that the future can hold abundant life rather than pervasive death, connectedness rather than isolation, health rather than disease, triumph rather than defeat. They cling to it for the promise of holistic salvation it offers them.

These poems, essays, and remembrances come from much the same places in which the books and stories of the Bible were created—oppression and exile. Similarly, these writings are exercises in resistance. They push back. They say no to efforts to instill shame or create fear. They make the strong claim that God loves LGBTQ people just as they are or despite the fact God may have made a mistake when their bodies were being shaped in the case of trans people.

Likewise, it should not be as surprising as it was for me that these writers, working out of their queerness, offer welcome new ways to think about major theological categories—creation, temptation, salvation, faith, hope, love. They offer welcome new ways to consider the characters in the Bible—Lot's wife, Abraham, Mary, Jesus, Lazarus, the wife of Cleopas. They offer inventive new ways to think about major biblical episodes—the fall, the flood, the annunciation, the crucifixion. In their close readings of the Bible, in their resistances, and in their inventiveness, they are playing a part in liberating themselves, liberating Christianity and the church, and liberating the Bible. They may even be liberating God.

Arranged by the chronological appearance of the author's selected verses in the Bible, *Rainbow in the Word* is organized into three parts. The first part, "Rainbow in the Old Testament," begins with Jeff Hood's freewheeling "Queering the Fall," the most theoretical piece in this collection. Hood believes that the bite of forbidden fruit is the most important moment in all of Scripture because, he says, that is where our queerness and God's queerness met. Tyler Heston in "The Outskirts of Sodom" offers a queer reading of Lot's wife. He draws an analogy between the unnamed woman and LGBTQ Christians who find themselves "frozen at the intersection of two supposed conflicting realities—sexual orientation and faith." In "Crossroads," Jonathan Freeman-Coppadge describes the moment when he found himself at a crossroads of faith and fear. Like Abraham, he had to choose between clinging to his previous understanding of God and his will or yielding to the voice of God which called him to come out as gay. Kenny Pierce, in "For Such a Time as This," relates the book of Esther to his own coming-of-age experiences. He raises a question for all LGBTQ Christians: "What if the real sin all along has been fighting our destiny and in walking away from our God-given purpose in a world made putrid under the weight of accusation and shame?" Because he has a soft spot for the underdog and the overlooked, Peterson Toscano identifies with the eunuchs in the Bible. In "Falling for Ebed Melech," he helps us to see eunuchs in the Bible not only as ones who refuse to be defeated but as ones, in Jeremiah's case, who may be saviors.

The second part of this collection consists of "Memories." The emphasis is on particular events in the writers' lives having little to do with the Bible per se but for which the Bible hovers in the background. It begins with three poems by Lisa A. Dordal. "The Lies that Save Us" opens with one of my favorite lines in this collection: "Driving through Georgia, we lie like Abraham." In "Commemoration," a two part memoir of her appearance in a Christmas pageant when she was twelve years old, Dordal lends feminist critique to the Virgin Birth story, and in "On the Road to Emmaus," she examines what it is like, as both a woman and a lesbian, to be invisible or "smoothed over by discourse." Kenny Pierce's "Stigmata" is a remembrance in two parts—"The Man on the Van Ness Bus" and "Lazarus." It is a confession that he gladly helped distribute safe-sex protection information about HIV/AIDS in bars and clubs during the early years of the pandemic, but looked the other way when a man covered with lesions got on a San Francisco bus one day and sat beside him.

Part three is "Rainbow in the New Testament." It begins with Riley Chattin's "Our Father," which describes the way he found the father he was needing in God as he transitioned from female to male and how, in the process, his relationship to the Lord's Prayer transitioned as well. With a dose of wit, Richard Barham, in "Good Fruit," plays off the gay slur against Jesus's response to the Pharisees that a good tree will necessarily bear good fruit. In "The Non-Normative Jesus," Andrew Dykstra invokes Jesus's teaching about the three kinds of eunuchs. He suggests Jesus was making a claim that Jesus was as non-normative as the eunuchs whom the Pharisees believed were excluded from the Covenant. In an inventive take on Jesus's cry, "My God, why have you forsaken me?", S. R. Davis, with her experience of having been born in the wrong body, confronts the idea that God doesn't make mistakes. Through readings of the flood and the crucifixion, she comes to see that God is intimately aware of the imperfections in creation. In "Magnificat: Seriously, God?" trans woman Jennifer Hasler tells how hearing Mary's story at an Advent service helped her to come out. In "My Great Hunger," Kenny Pierce traces his hard won new understanding of the command in the disciple Peter's vision: "Get up, Peter; kill and eat." After a long battle with personal demons, Pierce understood he was not to kill his homosexuality, he was to kill the false sense within him that he was unworthy of a seat at God's banquet table.

The memoirs turn to romantic love with Todd McGraw's "Prince Charming." Like so many other gay young men, McGraw believed he was unworthy of love. A fresh reading of 1 Cor 13, the Bible's so-called "love passage," however, was a game changer for him as he realized a primary challenge for him was patient, kind self love. Stephen V. Sprinkle examines 1 John in "Love Letter." He discovers that sensual love, truly divine love, takes place in the exchange of affection all people have with one another—including LGBTQ people. The final essay in this collection is Ray Jordan's "Revelation." Jordan carefully draws out the connection as he sees it between the assertion that "God is love" and the assertion in the last book of the Bible, the book of Revelation, that God, or love, is the "Alpha and Omega, the beginning and the end."

No matter where you are on the gender and sexuality scale, if you are a Christian (and maybe if you're not), you will find these new biblical readings to be fresh, captivating, and unexpected.

Ellin Sterne Jimmerson

PART I

Rainbow in the Old Testament

1

Queering the Fall

JEFF HOOD

So when the woman saw that the tree was good for food, and that it was
a delight to the eyes, and that the tree was to be desired to make one
wise, she took of its fruit and ate; and she also gave some to her husband,
who was with her, and he ate.

—GEN 3:6

IN THE BEGINNING . . . God created. Light joined the darkness.
Water separated. Sky formed. Land appeared. Vegetation sprang
forth. Stars were thrown into the sky. Moons were hung into place.
Fire appeared in the heavens. Creatures swarmed everywhere. In
spite of it all, something was missing. Creation was incomplete.
After much thought, humanity was created in the very image of
God. The story began.

Humanity was a full concept. No one was ever alone. The
Garden of Eden was a home for many. When God told them that
there was a deadly fruit tree in the middle of the Garden, they
asked the same question that anybody would: "Why would God

create a deadly fruit tree in the midst of such perfection?" Who cares that God told them not to eat it? God shouldn't have put it there in the first place. Nevertheless, somebody responded to the temptation and ate the damn fruit.

The bite of forbidden fruit is the most important moment in all of Scripture. Why did God put the tree there in the first place? Perhaps God knew that humanity would eat the fruit and wanted it to be that way.

Perhaps our response to temptation is what constitutes our creation in the image of God. Maybe temptation isn't always bad. Perhaps temptation is a mixed bag? How could eating a piece of fruit be such a deadly risk? God wanted us to be like God. God responded to God's temptation to not be alone by creating us. God interacts with temptation every moment. God is God based on God's responses to temptation. The temptation of God is always to cease being queer.

What makes humanity divine is our ability to emulate God and chart our own course in the midst of the temptations of life. There is nothing that is human without temptation. There is nothing that is divine without temptation.

In the midst of normativity, temptation unleashes the queer. Queerness is what makes us divine. We all have our own unique responses to temptation. If not for temptation we would be just like everybody else. If not for God's responses to temptation, God would not be God. God knew that we needed that fruit tree. The Fall is what makes us like God.

Do you ever think about aliens? Can you imagine what it would be like to find another world? What if we figured out that it was inhabited by intelligent life? What if we were able to go there? Once we made contact, we would lower the spaceship. When we were able to assure the inhabitants that we meant no harm, we would open the door. Slowly descending the stairs, we would look around.

What if we found a pre-fallen world? Temptation never hit the inhabitants. Maybe they were able to resist. Maybe God forgot the tree. Whatever the reason, we cannot believe our eyes. Looking around, it is impossible for us not to see that everyone is exactly the same. There is nothing unique about anyone. We quickly realize that temptation is what makes us queer. The normative beings that inhabit the planet find us to be sinful. The normative always dismisses the queer. Figuring that they have nothing to learn from us, the normative aliens just go back to their normative ways. We thought we found new life and quickly realized that all we had found was death.

I have often found myself back in Eden. Temptation has followed me throughout my life. For better or worse, how I've responded to temptation has made me who I am. I guess this is true of all of us. Divinity is found in the choosing.

Salvation is an interesting concept. We yearn to be saved and assume that we know the way to get there. The first humans were convinced that salvation was based on staying away from the fruit of a tree. It's interesting that sometimes what we assume to be salvation is actually death. The totality of God was found in temptation. God was found in rejecting concepts of normativity and embracing queerness. God is found in pushing back against concepts of salvation and embracing the queer.

Like many Christians, I grew up in a world full of the temptation of salvation. Every time we gathered, we were asked to come down the aisle. Every time we gathered, we were asked to pray a prayer. Every time we gathered, the temptation of salvation stalked us. We were told that we had to "Know that we know that we know that we know . . . that we are truly born again." The problem is that no one realized that salvation is not about knowing. Salvation is about being who God created us to be in the first place. Humanity discovered salvation when it overcame the temptation of salvation. Salvation is about being the queer.

God has never been about certainty. The temptation of certainty diminishes our lives. God created life to be about seeking. God is found in our seeking. How can we blame the humans in the Garden for seeking greater knowledge of God? Our certainties about the Fall are incredibly harmful. Humanity was trying to seek God. What could be more queer or divine than that?

Throughout my life, the temptation of certainty seems always to be close by. There was the time that I read the entire Bible to make sure I believed it all. When I made it through, I was no closer to certainty than I was when I started. There is something queer about reading the Bible as a mystery. I repeated prayers to be certain of my right standing with God. The prayers never helped. There is something queer about learning to pray with our being. Certainty isn't real . . . God is.

Identity is incredibly false. The temptation of identity is about being something other than what God has created us to be. We were created to be unique. We were created to be queer. When humanity rejected normativity and ate of the tree, humanity became unique and whole in its collective queerness. We must reject the temptation to be anything other than who we are. We must embrace who God created us to be by leading us to the tree.

We live in an age of identity. Everyone is trying to define who they are. Perhaps God is most fully found in rejecting the identities and being who one is. I never experienced wholeness until I started to live as a unique queer person. Queerness has never been about definitions. Queerness is about being. The first persons were normative until they expressed their queer individuality. Identity destroys individuality. The temptation of identity is always to reject who we are. Who are we? We are queers. We can thank the first persons for that. *Amen.*

2

The Outskirts of Sodom

TYLER HESTON

But Lot's wife, behind him, looked back, and she became a pillar of salt.

—GEN 19:26

For a long time, the Bible cleaved in two the reality of my faith and the reality of my burgeoning sexuality. At an early age, I believed firmly that the Bible and, therefore, God were opposed to queerness. A story in Genesis, a handful of abstract Biblical commandments, and a rhetorical argument at the beginning of Romans formed the painful belief that God did not want me to be gay. My coming out involved a difficult but rewarding period of theological transformation that began with a re-learning of the Bible.

Jeanette Winterson's novel, *Oranges Are Not the Only Fruit*, was a milestone in my theological transformation. Her novel tells the coming-of-age story of a young lesbian woman who grew up in an English Pentecostal community. This passage had a profound impact on how I interpreted the story of Lot's wife.

"Don't you ever think of going back?" Silly question. . . .
I'm always thinking of going back. When Lot's wife
looked over her shoulder, she turned into a pillar of salt.
Pillars hold things up, and salt keeps things clean, but it's
a poor exchange for losing your self. People do go back,
but they don't survive, because two realities are claiming
them at the same time.[1]

I was struck by how Winterson reimagined the classic Sodom
story—the story of Sodom's destruction was no longer a weapon
needing to be disassembled but a symbolic narrative for queer
Christians like me. Now, it is still difficult to return to this passage—once for me one of the "clobber passages"—without wincing
at old spiritual wounds they once inflicted.

Winterson helped me understand that queer biblical scholarship can unearth this passage's potential for empowering queer
Christians who know the pain of dueling realities. This text, a quick
subplot in the great drama of Abraham, momentarily spotlights
Lot's wife who perishes in a moment of hesitation during her flight
from Sodom into a new reality. For me, a queer reading of Lot's unnamed wife welcomes complexity. I now feel empathy for her; she is
no longer simply a foil to Lot's morality. Lot's wife is often a hallmark
of Old Testament disobedience, but I see her as caught in the cross-
fire of two realities—her residence in the unrighteous Sodom and
the calling and blessing given to her by the God of Abraham.

Why does Lot's wife glance back? What makes her doubt the
angels' warning to leave quickly? Is it curiosity or perhaps sor-
row from seeing destruction rain on her former home? Or is it a
spiteful look back, reveling in the end of a place that had denied
her true identity? Regardless of her motivation, she is the most fa-
mous casualty in the Pompeiian-like destruction brought to a city
of unrighteousness and compromised identity. How many queer
Christians likewise find themselves frozen at the intersection of
two supposed conflicting realities—sexual orientation and faith?

1. Jeannette Winterson, *Oranges Are Not the Only Fruit* (London: Pandora,
1985), 160.

So it was that, when God destroyed the cities of the Plain. . . . opens the abrupt, concluding verse of Sodom's story with the vivid imagery of *the smoke of the land going up like the smoke of a furnace* left in the reader's mind as a warning. The warning is often erroneously interpreted as one against sexual sin and the disastrous effects of feminine curiosity.

So it was that may be a sobering end to this narrative, but I believe that this somber tale is not a condemnation of queer Christians but rather a striking illustration of the ruinous duality in which many queer Christians exist. So it was that, when a town and its inhabitants were turned to ashes. So it was that, when Lot's wife was reduced to a pillar of salt. So it was that, when her family continued onward, broken, and moments away from more mishap.

So it is that, when queer Christians are forced into dual realities. So it is that, when queer Christians are forced to disassociate or be denied. So it is that, when queer Christians lose their divine destiny and do not know themselves as beloved children of God. Christianity that is opposed to queer folk is much like the outskirts of Sodom, a muddled place between God's grace and Sodomite chaos—a place that trapped Lot's wife as two realities claimed her at the same time.

Queer Christians are exhausted from defending themselves against the story of Sodom's usual clobber interpretations. Having once been lost in the outskirts of Sodom, I am grateful for the ways in which I now live honestly with myself, even though I sometimes do look back at past comforts and familiarities sacrificed in my coming out. I look back at the ease of having an unquestioned worldview that worked so long as I did not think too hard about my own attractions. I look back at my beloved childhood church community of which I could no longer be a true member because of my sexuality. To try to go back to the way things were, however, would be a poor exchange for losing myself.

Not all are as fortunate as I, and countless stories of queer Christians never able to embrace themselves stand like an arid desert of salt pillars, each a reminder of the dire need for Christianity to be open to all. A re-reading of the story of Lot's wife, aided by Winterson's novel, helped me realize that the ancient story of Sodom, the rest of the clobber passages, and the entirety of the Bible are not texts to be feared by queer Christians. Instead, these are our sacred Scriptures too, beckoning us into holy conversation, breathing life into our spirituality, and offering words to our own experiences as beloved people of God.

3

Crossroads

Jonathan Freeman-Coppadge

When they came to the place that God had shown him, Abraham built
an altar there and laid the wood in order. He bound his son Isaac, and
laid him on the altar, on top of the wood. Then Abraham reached out his
hand and took the knife to kill his son. But the angel of the Lord called
to him from heaven, and said, "Abraham, Abraham!" And he said, "Here
I am." He said, "Do not lay your hand on the boy or do anything to him;
for now I know that you fear God, since you have not withheld your son,
your only son, from me."

—Gen 22:9–12

I was raised in a strongly biblical, Plymouth Brethren family, a
tradition in which the label "fundamentalist" was a badge of
honor. Until the age of twenty-one, I dealt with my sexual orientation through avoidance. I thought I could hold my desires at bay,
suppress them, starve them on a diet of prayer.

It wasn't until an autumn weekend of my senior year in college that I faced the truth of my sexuality. I was supposed to be

driving to West Virginia for a church retreat, but first I decided to visit a friend who had seemed depressed earlier that day. Over the next half-hour, he told me about coming to terms with his own same-sex attractions, about his fears of how his friends would treat him, what his Catholic parents would think, and what it all meant for his future. I had been in prayer from the moment I walked in and, when he finished speaking, I knew I had to reciprocate that trust and confide in him. For the first time ever, I vocalized my attractions and my own confusion about what to do with them. Strangely, I was perfectly calm while I was talking and, an hour later, I climbed in my car and headed off to West Virginia.

My world fell apart during that two-hour drive. The reality of what I had confessed suddenly hit me—this could change or destroy all that I held dear. It was no longer a sneaking suspicion that I could ignore and deny; it was an objective reality that someone else knew about. By the time I reached West Virginia around midnight, I was despondent. I spent that weekend trying to pull myself together and the next year in fervent soul searching.

After I graduated, my family spent a week on Grindstone Island in New York. It is the kind of place where you can hear the dialogue of your own soul with God as the noise of life is washed away by the St. Lawrence River. One morning I decided to read and pray before breakfast. I found a boulder by the riverside and opened to the familiar story of Abraham and Isaac. But this time I realized that the stumbling block for Abraham lay not just in the sacrifice of his only son, but it lay also in the very nature of God's request. The sacrifice of a child was something required by the gods of those people around Abraham, the kind abhorred by the God whose nature never changes. The request directly contravened Abraham's understanding of who God is and what he desires. Abraham was forced to decide between clinging to his previous understanding of God and his will, or yielding to the voice that called him to do something he could not understand. Abraham chose faith over certainty.

I sat on the rock, deep in prayer. And in the quiet, I heard a very clear question:

If I were calling you to live your life as a gay man, would you follow me in faith or would you cling to what you think you know about me? Would you say, "Lead, Lord, and I will follow," or would you say, "You simply couldn't be asking me to do that. I refuse"? Would you yield to my voice, or would you try to tell me what I can and cannot ask of you?

My response on that day was honest: "I want to be able to say that I would follow you anywhere, whether I understood it or not. But I cannot honestly say that I am there yet. I am too scared of what I have to lose. I fear I will lose my family. I want to have the faith to follow you, but my fear still has a grip on me. My spirit is willing, but my flesh is weak."

God's response: *That is enough for now.*

I spent the next few years stripping away the voices of fear and trying to hear the still, small voice of God. The cries of condemnation were loud in my head, but I clung to the promise that there is no condemnation for those who are in Christ Jesus. I approached the throne of grace with humbleness and trembling, but also with the confidence that I was seeking the will of the one who made me and knew me before the world began and that he would keep my feet from falling. When I was finally able to remove the obstacles of fear that fought to interpose themselves between God and me, when we were left alone in my heart to talk, my conscience did not condemn me, and I felt a sense of blessing on my desire to be in a loving, committed relationship.

I realized, too, that if I chose to run away from that desire, if I pursued a life of celibacy, I would be doing it not out of a sense of God's calling but out of the fear of what I would lose by embracing my orientation. I did not understand how God could bless a gay relationship, but I did know that whatever is not done in faith is sin. I was at a crossroads of faith and fear, and I stepped forward in faith, recognizing that I was possibly being asked to leave home and brothers and father and mother to answer the calling, trusting that I would also touch the promises Jesus offered. Like Abraham, I was being called to say yes to God despite the fact that I did not understand the request, despite the fact that it flew in the face of my previous understanding of God.

I do not think my story is typical, but today, in the company of my husband, son, parents, and siblings, I testify that there is, in fact, a promised land to which we are called. Choosing the way of faith brought me into its riches.

4

For Such a Time as This

KENNY PIERCE

For if you keep silence at such a time as this, relief and deliverance will rise for the Jews from another quarter, but you and your father's family will perish. Who knows? Perhaps you have come to royal dignity for just such a time as this.

—ESTH 4:14

For those living in marginalized groups, their life stories—the sum of their life's narrative—often feel irrelevant in a time of seemingly endless darkness and division in the world. This passage from the book of Esther was on my mind driving home one night from the sharing of transformative stories with friends in my tribe of gay Christian men.

Myself and so many others in this and in the other groups comprising the LGBTQ community have lived our lives under the thumb of institutions telling us that how we were created—all that we've ever known and understood ourselves to be—is an abomination. There isn't a single one of us that remembers choosing our sexual orientations or gender identities as so many tell us we've done, and yet we all bought into the lies and into the shame. We believed that our very nature was a sin, that somehow God made a series of radical mistakes in creating us.

We've been bullied; we've been forced into reparative therapy. We've been told that things like the AIDS pandemic or gay bashings that I've born witness to were God's retribution (or "nature's revenge" to use the 1983 words of Pat Buchanan, Ronald Reagan's communications director, to describe the AIDS scourge) that we brought upon ourselves. In countries such as Iran, Nigeria, Saudi Arabia, and Afghanistan, homosexuality is a crime that carries with it the penalty of death. The more humane among us may shudder at news coverage of gay men in these countries being pushed off of buildings and assume ourselves to be culturally superior, yet we'd do well to remember that it was only in 1973 (my ninth year on this planet) that the American Psychological Association removed homosexuality from its *Diagnostic and Statistical Manual of Mental Disorders*. Prior to this, however, one could legally be forced into reparative therapy or be institutionalized by disapproving family and friends without recourse. These sorts of memories are among many that have produced the scars worn by so many of our elders in the LGBTQ community. Addiction, suicide, self-loathing, and mental illness have been the fruit of a rotten tree, one rooted in shame and accusation flung at us from every corner and from the highest levels of human authority.

A Christian friend once reminded me gently, when I was in a fit of despair over my own sexuality, that shame is never of God and that Satan was once called the Great Accuser. The satanic violence of relentless accusations and shaming tactics that have tried to crush us to the core have become internalized in toxic ways. The violence of those accusations has become transformed into an internal violence of shame, of the unending, seemingly irremediable but false sense that who we are is fundamentally wrong and can never be put right. We should have been eradicated long ago by a supposed blood-thirsty god, and yet here we are.

And so, as I was driving home from this particular support group meeting that night, an intriguing thought that arose from our conversation wouldn't leave me. What if the real sin all along has been our fighting the very nature that God designed? What if there is a very real purpose for our being on this earth—something that we're meant to teach? What if, for all of our desires to check out along the way in one way or another, what if for all of our feeling that our lives were wasted in the face of such condemnation by the church, what if, instead, God had something quite distinct in mind, something that would work through our lives to teach the rest of humankind?

What if the real sin all along has been fighting our destiny and in walking away from our God-given purpose in a world made putrid under the weight of accusation and shame?

I've said many times that I've seen true holiness play out twice in my life: first, through the way our community lifted one another during the peak of the AIDS pandemic in America; and second, how those of us who are struggling in recovery from addictions let our stories work for the betterment of others similarly struggling to stay clean and sober. The key to such holiness in both cases has been our being courageous and honest enough to share our stories openly, to let God's grace work through us, to set ourselves aside for the sake of our falling or fallen brothers and sisters.

It is no longer the 1980s and 1990s, and it is now eighteen years since I took my last drink. In 2017, I now find myself living through a time of scapegoating, of marginalization, of divisions in the world that seem to emanate from an endless river of darkness, and yet I've seen so much light and holiness that I know better than to give up hope. With the gifts of wisdom and insight that the years engender in those of us lucky enough to survive our various wars in this world, I've come to believe that the great sin on the part of our community—and the larger church and society that would stifle this very nature that God created—is that of silencing our stories. The great sin resides in buying the lie that it was all for naught. No, I've increasingly come to understand that this wounded world desperately needs us and the lessons that we have to offer.

I believe that we, the people who make up the LGBTQ community, are far more than our libidos or our gender expressions. I'm reminded of some indigenous communities that exalted members of their communities who were thought to traverse multiple gender realms. Some in the Lakota, the Ojibwe, and the Navajo nations saw this nature as gifts of healing abilities and of spiritual wisdom—quite the antithesis of a curse or sin that mainstream Western secular and religious societies attempt to ingrain in us. Speaking personally and looking back at my own life with this model in mind, it is true that I've felt myself able to understand and connect deeply with the two spirits spoken of by such traditions, that of the masculine and feminine running within, and have often called on both when empathy, compassion, and understanding were most demanded of me. I've come to cherish this, my nature, as just such a blessed gift.

It is long past the lessons in holiness that I learned from AIDS and from addiction to alcohol. It is 2017, and I believe that in a world as dark as what we're living through now, in the age of the demonic forces that gave rise to leaders who would stoke fear and hatred to galvanize their positions and their base, I believe that it's no accident that acceptance of members of LGBTQ people is increasing.

This might come as a surprise to those who feel as if the ground is swallowing them up in a vat of homophobia. No, I've seen far worse and lived through times when affirmation was a nonstarter. This is something different. Knowing the kind of holiness that unfolded before me in years past, from the unlikeliest of places, I believe that we have much to teach. Who better to do so than those who've endured so much, who understand pain so well? We have much to heal in this broken world, much work to do. I believe that as two spirit people, God brought us here to do this sacred healing work. That some are fighting this healing so vehemently speaks more to the nature of demonic darkness and its unwillingness to relinquish the reigns of control than it does to how we're viewed by God.

5

Falling for Ebed Melech

Peterson Toscano

Ebed-melech the Ethiopian, a eunuch in the king's house, heard that they had put Jeremiah into the cistern. The king happened to be sitting at the Benjamin Gate, So Ebed-melech left the king's house and spoke to the king, "My lord king, these men have acted wickedly in all they did to the prophet Jeremiah by throwing him into the cistern to die there of hunger, for there is no bread left in the city." Then the king commanded Ebed-melech the Ethiopian, "Take three men with you from here, and pull the prophet Jeremiah up from the cistern before he dies."

—Jer 38:7–10

I feel drawn to eunuchs in the Bible. I recognize something in them—their outsider status. I felt like an outsider in the many churches I have attended. Growing up, I received a powerful message broadcasted on the playground, in the press, and especially from the pulpit—*You would be fully welcome and valuable if you were heterosexual and masculine.*

I was a gay boy in an anti-LGBTQ society. As a result, I dove into the weird and dangerous world of conversion therapies and submitted to seventeen years of ex-gay ministries. Even with all my efforts to "de-gay" myself, I remained an outsider. In a world that valued male leadership, I was not straight enough or masculine enough to lead as a minister or teacher. Nevertheless, pastors regularly turned to me for my creativity and communication skills. They would not allow me to preach my own sermons, but they would happily let me give them material for theirs.

When I finally came to my senses and came out gay, I refused to toss out the Baby Jesus and the Bible with the anti-LGBTQ bathwater. I began to discover Bible characters routinely left out of the abridged versions of Bible stories preached from the pulpit. It was through this creative dialogue with the Bible that I fell hard for eunuchs.

In Bible stories, eunuchs are usually foreigners. They are also gender and sexual minorities. Castrated as boys, they never experience puberty. Without testosterone coursing through them, they retain high voices, smooth beardless faces, and minimal body hair and muscle mass. Eunuchs cannot produce children. They look and sound different from the men and women around them. They are seen as neither children nor adults, male nor female. Something in the middle or altogether different, they live in the cracks.

These eunuchs pop up in many Bible stories and are usually ignored in the retelling of these narratives. Typically, in both liberal and conservative churches, when a preacher references the Book of Esther, we only hear about the non-eunuchs—Hadassah/ Esther, her kinsman Mordecai, King Xerxes, and Hamman, the evil henchman who attempts to murder all the Jews. We sometimes also hear about Queen Vashti, a strong female character who has the audacity to say "No" to a man.

While these non-eunuch characters are familiar to many ministers and churchgoers, most people cannot name any of the twelve eunuchs who appear in the Book of Esther. These eunuchs effortlessly move in and out of the palace, through male and female spaces, royal quarters, and common back streets. They have diverse roles in the palace—guards, soldiers, advisers, assassins, surrogate parents, beauty and etiquette consultants, sex experts, servants, and, as most commonly remarked upon, overseers of the royal harem.

Take these eunuchs out of the story of Esther, and the entire narrative falls apart. While God is never once mentioned in the eleven chapters of Esther, these twelve eunuchs drive the action throughout. That is why when I tell the story of Esther, I always reference at least one of these eunuchs: Mehuman, Biztha, Harbona, Bigtha, Abagtha, Zethar, Carcas, Shaashgaz, Teresh, Bigthana, Hathach, and my favorite, Hegai. Hegai becomes a surrogate parent to the orphaned exile Esther and gives her a special beauty treatment along with inside information about what to bring into the bedroom when it is time to visit the king.

One of the eunuch stories that moves me the most appears in the book of Jeremiah. Ebed Melech, a eunuch in the royal court of Judah, is an African from Cush or modern day Ethiopia/Eritrea.

Jeremiah calls on the nation to repent or else suffer the consequences. Instead of heeding the warning, some in the ruling party capture the prophet, drag him into the palace, drop him into an empty muddy well, and leave him there to die.

King Zedekiah, who is sympathetic toward Jeremiah, doesn't have any real power in the court to help his friend. Perhaps someone who is often overlooked in the palace can assist? Enter Ebed Melech. This Ethiopian eunuch goes directly to King Zedekiah and urges action. As a result, the King of Judah gives Ebed Melech some fighting men so they can rescue Jeremiah.

Ebed Melech organizes a Special Ops midnight raid to "Navy-seal" Jeremiah out of the muddy well and the palace. This foreign-born court official thinks of everything, including rope to haul Jeremiah up from the well. The rescue team also bring with them old rags. These the eunuch tosses down to the prophet and whispers, "Put these rags under your arms, so when we pull you up, the rope won't cut or burn your skin." This Ethiopian eunuch saves the old man prophet. This often overlooked Black, African, surgically altered, and gender variant eunuch becomes a savior. Ebed Melech changes the course of both the narrative and prophetic history.

Without him, Jeremiah and his prophetic judgements would have perished in the muddy cistern.

Being an outsider—a gay Christian—has been painful and alienating. I escaped anti-LGBTQ churches and continue to work through the trauma of religious abuse. I am still undoing the harm from the all those years when ministers armed me with biblical weapons designed to destroy my own sexuality and self. Before I came out, I felt the need to live in the cracks and conceal parts of myself in order to survive. There was a time that squeezing my quirky, queer self into those tight oppressive spaces felt necessary. Not anymore.

Perhaps that is why I have a soft spot for the underdog and the overlooked, especially those who press up against the walls constructed around them. I read about biblical eunuchs and see people who refuse to be defeated. They deploy their creativity, ambition, even their differences, not only to make a way for themselves, but to make the world a better place.

PART II

Memories

6

Three Poems

LISA A. DORDAL

THE LIES THAT SAVE US

From there Abraham journeyed toward the region of the Negeb, and settled between Kadesh and Shur. While residing in Gerar as an alien, Abraham said of his wife Sarah, "She is my sister." And King Abimelech of Gerar sent and took Sarah.

—GEN 20:1–2

Driving through Georgia,
we lie like Abraham.
Are you sisters?, people ask.
Yes, we answer. *Twins, even.*
Though we are dressed similarly
in broad-brimmed hats,
long-sleeved shirts, and tan pants
tucked into thick, white socks
(it being tick season and all)—

we look nothing alike.
Thought so, people say,
as if they have figured out
some secret code. We smile back,
knowing the power of things unseen:
of atoms, quarks, and auras
and all the love that lies between.
Kissing energy, we call it.
But all they can see is
something.[1]

COMMEMORATION

Mary said to the angel, "How can this be, since I am a virgin?" The angel said to her, "The Holy Spirit will come upon you, and the power of the Most High will overshadow you; therefore the child to be born will be holy; he will be called Son of God."

—LUKE 1:34–35

Christmas Pageant

At twelve, I played Mary
in a community Christmas pageant.
I saw you at the service, people said.
I saw you with your baby,
riding your donkey. A real donkey,
led by some boy. Older boy.
Fourteen at least. I don't remember
his name or if I even knew it
at the time. Just that I couldn't look at him.
Couldn't look straight at him

1. "The Lies that Save Us" first appeared in *Bridges: A Jewish Feminist Journal* 12 (2007) 60.

without blushing and lowering my eyes.
Everyone said I made a great Mary.
That I did a great job being
the one God descended upon. No,
not descended upon. Entered.
That I did a great job being the one
God entered. And who
afterwards called it holy.

Christmas Pageant Revisited

The boy is important, the visiting poet said.
Immensely important. The center of the poem,
he said. Her desire for him is the center of the poem,
the *dramatic* center. Her desire for him is
what this poem is about. This much is clear:
She *desires* him. The girl riding a donkey
desires him, the boy, the dramatic center.
You need to build him up more,
he continued. Give him a name, good looks,
maybe a touch of acne. Help us to see him,
to see the real center of this poem.
To see *into* the center; to see inside her
desire. Help us to get inside—
inside the blushing and the lowering.
Tell us how blue his eyes are, how dark his hair,
how straight and perfect his
nose. We need to *see* him. The center
of her desire. Unless, of course, you are striving
(*striving!*) to create an aura of mystery—
an *illusion* of mystery—like you would
if you were talking about, say, God.[2]

2. "Commemoration" first appeared in *Journal of Feminist Studies in Religion* 26 (Spring 2010) 121.

ON THE WAY TO EMMAUS

While they were talking and discussing, Jesus himself came near but their eyes were kept from recognizing him. One of them, named Cleopas, asked, "Are you the only stranger in Jerusalem who does not know the things that have happened there in these days?"

—LUKE 24:14–18

It's easy to see Jesus. We can't
not see him with his thick carpenter arms,
hair the color of Galilee night,
eyes vexed with knowing.
Jesus himself came near.

But you we do not see: the woman,
the wife, the one with Cleopas. You,
the stranger, we do not see, still.

I know what it's like not to be seen;
what it's like to be smoothed over by discourse;
to have the bumpy parts gone,
your own rich texture of being
dulled into round slivers of yearning,
a dark, holy heaviness lost:
the year I taught New Testament—
Paul, the Gospels, Revelation—
and everyone thought I was straight.
You foolish Galatians!, I began,
continuing with the offspring
of Christ, the curse of the law,
and the knife that Paul hopes will slip.
Until the last day, when I came out—
one part Christian, one part Jew, all queer.

I know what it's like not to be seen
but, still, my eyes faltered and all I saw
was two men walking, one of whom,
true stranger in the text, was you.[3]

3. "On the Way to Emmaus" first appeared in *Journal of Feminist Studies in Religion* 25 (Fall 2009) 88.

7

A Remembrance in Two Parts

KENNY PIERCE

From the sole of the foot even to the head, there is no soundness in it, but bruises and sores and raw wounds; they are not pressed out or bound up or softened with oil.

—ISA 1:6

STIGMATAS

The Man on the Van Ness Bus

There is a thorn. A kind of stigmata that eats me from within that will not heal. I am ashamed. I, like so many others. Once, twice, a multitude of times. We all looked away. We stared at anything but the ugliness around us. Perhaps it was a survival mechanism, to keep ourselves sane.

But we looked away, while all the while we chanted the mantra taught to us, again and again:

Silence = Death.

Our marching orders: to make our plight known. We would illuminate the silence, the darkness, with this battle cry. I knew these words well, and our chorus rang out in those streets where the blood of my fallen brothers and sisters ran through the gutters to the drains. To their ultimate destination. *We sang to end the silence. To do something. Somebody had to do something.*

I suppose that I could have assumed the role of nurse to the dying. I could have been closer to that which I was fighting. Yet I much preferred more palatable sights. Many of us did, as we hit our crescendos. As we walked the bars and cafes proclaiming the word of our own immediate salvation. *We sought desperately to save ourselves. To find a way to save each other.*

"Will you sign up? How much do you know about safe sex? We'll be holding a meeting this week. If you wouldn't mind attending. . . . Oh you will? That's great. Could I get your name and number? How about condoms? Are you good for the night? OK, well here. Here's a handful. USE THEM! And behave yourself."

This was rather fun. Meeting people this way, and he was kind of cute. I wondered if he'd be there on Tuesday night.

He said that he's still negative. Thank God for that. *Thank God that someone was taking care of the dying this way. Thank God for us.*

When I climbed on the Van Ness bus heading north that fall day in 1991 in San Francisco, it was almost lunchtime. I was thinking about whether I'd stop at the culinary school for lunch or ride up to the Marina.

I was in my own world when I noticed him climb onto the bus and take a spot up front across from me. He was so worn and thin, he was barely able to walk to his seat. He turned his head my way.

I caught a glance at what, at one time, must have been the most beautiful eyes. But staring back at me now were the waning lights of two dying candle wicks awaiting the final gust of wind that would extinguish them.

The lesions were all over him. Kaposi's sarcoma.

The shirt that hung so oversized and loose on his ninety-pound frame couldn't conceal the giant purple ovals. They were the wounds of a thousand nails pounded into him. It occurred to me that he was covered in his own universe of agonizing stigmatas.

"Act normally, Kenny. Oh, God he's staring." I caught his glance and his eyes were begging, filled with such need. But what did he want? Did he just want to be seen again? Did he just want to be beautiful, free of the festering wounds? If only for ten minutes more?

"What does he want?"

I couldn't see. Dear God, forgive me but I didn't want to see, and I looked away.

He was real. It was all so suddenly real, and there it was beside me.

His wounds became my own as he looked on, hollow-eyed. My eyes were opened abruptly. Before me was the agonizing pain of my brother in the gay community dying of AIDS.

I was new to The City and those who died up until that time did so quickly. Out of sight, in the abstract.

One day they were the glorious and the mighty in the bars and in the gyms. A year later, their praises were sung in the obituaries that I'd flip through as I was grabbing a bite to eat. I'd see the faces. I'd walk to fight the disease. I knew that they'd died, but it wasn't real.

Though the headlines announced it all.

This man or that. Young twenty, thirty, forty-year-olds. *He bravely fought, but succumbed to AIDS.*

They all bravely fought the civil war that raged within them. And those like me still on the sidelines were meant to tend to the fallen. That was our post.

And what a coward I was. I left my post, hopped on a bus, and kept my gaze down.

What became of the skeleton across from me on that bus? One among dozens that must have passed each other on the streets of The City every day. Did they nod one to the other or did they also look away at the reflections of themselves in the mirrors that passed before them?

Yes I, like others, was polite and looked away. "Better not to stare, to make them feel self-conscious" everyone recoiling told themselves.

Better to make him invisible as he waits for his stop.

Who attended the lesions that covered him when he arrived home? When iron rivets were driven into his legs, his arms, his head. His was a crown of thorns born of silence amidst the disease and the wounds that festered in no small part a result of the apathy of others.

And I . . . running from one bar to another, making certain that the pretty boys received their protection for the night. Sign them up. Bring them in. But be sure that they're pretty. I gravitated to the pretty but what was before me was anything but. Perhaps in his time, I would have eagerly approached him as well. Before I, like others, rendered him invisible.

Lazarus

When he had said this, he cried with a loud voice, "Lazarus, come out!" The dead man came out, his hands and feet bound with strips of cloth, and his face wrapped in a cloth. Jesus said to them, "Unbind him, and let him go."

—JOHN 11:43–44

Some rose from the threshold of death when the worst was past.

Some of us never really fell.

How could I speak haughtily of God's grace shown to me? Oh, yes, he did indeed keep me safe. Yet so many who lost those who were most precious to them clung to trinkets of their dead. Their fights were far more ferocious.

Why not me?

It is 2016.

I survived the nightmare, to test positive for HIV thirteen years ago.

I take the pills twice a day now.

"I think that we should start you on medication. Your numbers are still OK, but your immune system is working in overdrive. I'll give you something that's well-tolerated. One in the morning. Two at night. Would you have any problems taking them twice during the day?"

Why not me?

Twice a day. I'm reminded twice a day of a grace afforded me, withheld to those who towered in stature and in courage. Our lost.

After 1997, there were many who were given the name Lazarus. Brought back from the brink by the bevy of new pills. They made it. They would have one, two, perhaps more decades.

They were given the blessing of time.

It is 2016 and what haunts me most is the man on the Van Ness bus.

What became of him? Where is he now? Did he make it?

By some miracle did he make it to live with the stigma but free of the stigmata (like those of us alive now)? Or did he walk to his bed, close his eyes, and open them to find them filled with the light of a new eternity?

Did a grave await him? Or did a trash bag as was common in those earliest days?

What became of that man? Thirty-five perhaps forty years old. Maybe sixty. It was so hard to tell. I would love to believe that he lived to be called Lazarus, too.

I still see him growing smaller in the distance as we rode further and further away from his stop.

Was he always so small? Or was he once great and mighty as were so many others?

My eyes still squint from the double paned window of that bus. The reflection that I see—that of myself—hurts my eyes and glares back at me.

I wear a coat of lesions inside of me now. Thorns that rip at my heart, that can never be touched, never assuaged. I live amidst the residual stigma that remains. Will they reject me, not come near me? Could I be loved by another?

What has defined us all for three decades courses through my veins, but the name Lazarus will never be mine to own.

For all that I never really faced, I am not worthy. But most particularly, for my indifference to my dying brother who rode that bus with me that day, who came to represent all that I never experienced, never suffered in the way that others did, never lost, and most importantly, all whose desperate gazes I avoided. For love of that man on the bus, I am not worthy.

I accepted the grace that saw me through. One that I didn't earn. But I can never be worthy to stand among the risen.

Lazarus.

I never wore the stigmata as they did. I can never be worthy of that name.

PART III

Rainbow in the New Testament

8

Our Father

RILEY CHATTIN

Pray then in this way: Our Father in heaven, hallowed be your name. Your kingdom come. Your will be done, on earth as it is in heaven. Give us this day our daily bread. And forgive us our trespasses, as we forgive those who trespass against us. And do not bring us to the time of trial, but rescue us from the evil one.

—MATT 6:9–13

T he Lord's Prayer and I go way back, not in the way one would think because I detested hearing or speaking it. While hearing the Lord's Prayer spoken simultaneously in our native languages at the National Cathedral in Washington, DC, I was able to let go of my aversion to it. Hearing it there in many languages made me aware of how we arrive at faith along different paths. The Lord's Prayer became, for me, a meditation on our journey as humans with divine possibilities.

Grace is not often part of my or other transgender individuals' experience, which includes berating, physical violence, and social isolation. Transgender children are often abandoned by their families. When I was eighteen, I came out as a lesbian. My mother called the police, and I was escorted out of my own house. My dad was the only family that spoke to me. At forty, when I legally changed my name and gender, out of respect for Mom who gave birth to me, I sent her a letter to let her know. There was not a relationship there. It was more for myself and for speaking the truth I had expressed as a child and a teenager—the awareness of being a boy. My father died a little over two years before I began to transition genders. This left me without a male figure in my life to turn toward. I craved a male figure to connect with, to be a guide through uncertain times of life. When those I tried to turn to learned I was a transgender man, none was available. Then I turned toward God, finding *My Father* within the Lord's Prayer.

Now, I speak *Our Father* in salutation to the creator of who I am and of our universe, of whom I and everyone around me share an atom of creation. However, this is more than a salutation, it is where I begin with God, universally whole as seen in the Trinity of the Father, Son, and Holy Spirit. This is one way I link to the universal energy of grace experienced through the Trinity.

Hallowed be your name. Since Our Father knows our worth before we do, declaring the hallowedness of his name feels, to me, like a call to action from God to live and help others to live in peace as we accept ourselves and come out.

Our Father is a father of grace, peace, and mercy. He placed an atom of light within us not outside of us. One way, I believe, that we can show this atom of light within us is to allow it to become outward in our physical transition. That is how it worked for me. Our Father gave me the courage to seek just what I needed to ease the spiritual discomfort I was feeling because of my body.

I find connection to others when I recite *Thy kingdom come, thy will be done. On Earth as it is in Heaven.* I strive to live together on Earth just as in Heaven with everyone even though each of our bodies is unique and different from others' bodies. It is like the mansion that has many rooms about which the Gospel writer John spoke (John 14:2). Our common Father created each of us divinely different from one another just as rooms and private spaces of our houses are unique yet part of a whole. For transgender people like me, we have to change our bodies just as we sometimes have to rearrange a room in order to be at rest spiritually. However, we remain a sacred creation of God, Our Father.

Many transgender people still seek basic needs, services, and safety. It once made me feel empty to speak of Heaven and Earth while reciting the Lord's Prayer. It seemed contrary to my experience to say, *Give us this day our daily bread.* When I had my "aha" moment in the National Cathedral that day, I realized that my daily bread came in the form of supportive friends, family, or a stranger affirming my gender identity. My needs continue each day, but I gain strength by accepting what is offered to me which helps me through another day.

And forgive us our trespasses as we forgive those who trespass against us. I, like all transgender people, have abundant opportunity to understand forgiveness of others who have hurt me with their actions while others turned their backs on me or ignored my mistreatment.

The forgiveness Our Father offered abundantly, however, includes the forgiveness I learned to give myself. I try to offer compassion to myself when I encounter discrimination or inequity. I take time to heal from the disrespect I experience almost daily. I do not accept limitations others try to put on me or deny myself an opportunity at life. It heals me to know that God made me, that I am his child, even though many tell me I am less than a child of God.

While I may know that God is my father, I encounter some who may not hold that same understanding. So, I ask for this help: *And do not bring us to the time of trial, but rescue us from the evil one.* While trials can be harm inflicted upon me, the temptation not to be an outcast is also a trial. I know it is up to me to hold on to the courage to live as my true self.

Jesus gave the Lord's Prayer to his disciples as an example of how to pray throughout their lives. We, as baptized Christians, are today's disciples including those of us who are transgender or other LGBQ people. We are repeatedly reminded in scripture not to be afraid. God knows it is not easy to live as our true selves when we are so different from the majority. I, as a transgender person, have been given the strength to openly confess that God is My Father and that I am part of his sacred creation. I know that I have the potential to live openly in this truth. How do I know it? The Bible tells me so.

9

Good Fruit

Richard Barham

Either make the tree good, and its fruit good; or make the tree bad, and
its fruit bad; for the tree is known by its fruit.

—Matt 12:33

In earlier days, the word "fruit" was a derogatory term used as
a gay slur. But it was Jesus's use of the word "fruit" that transformed its meaning from a derogatory one to a complimentary
one in my life. Jesus's fruit tree teaching became a pivotal moment
in my life and ministry. It is amazing to me that in just a couple
of sentences, Jesus reversed years of questioning and doubt with
confirmation and faith.

I was born into a deeply rooted Southern Baptist family.
Church was part and parcel of my life from the very beginning.
I accepted Jesus Christ as my Savior and Lord when I was seven
years old. I was always a part of my Sunday school and discipleship
training (or Training Union for the Southern Baptist old school-
ers). Instead of being a Boy Scout, I was a Royal Ambassador, the

Southern Baptist version of the Boy Scouts. And then my involvement became ever greater with my church's youth group. I think a person can quickly get a picture of what my childhood and teenage years were like. There was no doubt in regards to my salvation experience and discipleship journey.

Despite a speech impediment, I felt a calling to be a preacher. After a time of discernment, I surrendered to God's call in my life. Once I did, the speech impediment pretty much went away and I have been preaching and pastoring on a consistent basis since the age of fifteen. There was no doubt in regards to my calling and vocational decision.

But I had a secret. I was gay. Just as I had no doubts in regard to my salvation, discipleship, and vocational calling, I also had no doubts that I was gay. Out of fear, I did not study the biblical passages that were used to condemn homosexuality. I knew what the church's teaching was. So I did what many do when conflicted—I tried to ignore it.

Since I had always been good at compartmentalization, I was able to move forward. I continued to preach, work in church ministry, go to seminary, accept pastorates, and yes, even date. At one point, I almost proposed to a wonderful young woman. But knowing my secret, I never summoned the courage to pop the question. As I matured, it became harder to keep everything compartmentalized. I was miserable. I was wearing a mask of heterosexuality. And as the warning label on all Halloween costumes makes clear, masks when worn for a long time will suffocate. I continued to ignore the biblical clobber passages out of fear. I was afraid that I would have to leave the ministry. I was afraid that maybe the church was right, and I had been deceived in thinking I was a Christian. My compartmentalization strategy was waning and the future was looking hopeless.

Little did I know that God had an epiphany moment in store for me. I was preparing a lesson based on Matt 12 where the Pharisees were making judgments about who and what was of God and who and what was not. In actuality, they were making those judgments about Jesus. In response to the Pharisees, Jesus says, "A tree is identified by its fruit. If a tree is good, its fruit will be good. If a tree is bad, its fruit will be bad."

I had read, studied, preached, and taught on Jesus's fruit tree lecture many times but now, for the first time, it became personal. For in that moment, it seemed that God was addressing me and my secret. As I have already made clear, I knew of my relationship with God. I knew of my calling to the ministry. And I also knew I had good fruit in my life and in my ministry. I asked the question to myself, "How could I have good fruit but yet be, according to the church's traditional teachings, a detestable pervert who was doomed to hell with no place for ministry?" According to Jesus, good fruit comes only from a good tree.

That epiphany moment had turned into an eureka moment. I was a good tree and better yet, as a gay man, a good fruity tree! While I was still a couple of years from being at peace with the integration of my homosexuality and Christianity, this moment of revelation about fruit trees gave me the courage to revisit those clobber passages. I soon discovered that the Bible does not condemn homosexuality as we know it today. Once that discovery was made, the mask that was suffocating me was taken off and I was free. Jesus's words about fruit trees had truly become, as the old hymn states, "wonderful words of life."

Today I am an out gay pastor who has been blessed with over twenty years of LGBTQ-affirming, Christ-centered ministry. When I teach my classes on the Bible and homosexuality, I always encourage those who are struggling to integrate their homosexuality and their Christianity not to be afraid to engage the Scriptures and ask the tough questions. But I also encourage them to engage the Scriptures and to wrestle with the church's traditional teachings with the knowledge and confidence that they are indeed a good tree. My prayer is they too will discover that what the world meant to be a gay slur, God has meant for the good.

10

The Non-Normative Jesus

ANDREW DYKSTRA

But he said to them, "Not everyone can accept this teaching, but only those to whom it is given. For there are eunuchs who have been so from birth, and there are eunuchs who have been made eunuchs by others, and there are eunuchs who have made themselves eunuchs for the sake of the kingdom of heaven. Let anyone accept this who can."

—MATT 19:12

For many years I struggled with comments Jesus made about heterosexual marriage as recorded in Matt 19. I felt excluded, through no fault of my own, from what his words seemed to prescribe. Ever since I was a teen, I felt that I could never marry anyone of the opposite sex. I knew I was gay, didn't understand why I was different, and was too afraid to ask for help because of my fear and shame. One day, I realized I had been reading the passage from the perspective of one who is heterosexual and normative, a perspective that was not helpful to me, a gay man. When I started to read the same chapter from my perspective as a gay man and thus non-normative, I discovered something startlingly new to me. It called into question my exclusionary reading of Matt 19. Jesus challenged the hardheartedness of the specialists in Mosaic Law by his surprising contrast of those Pharisees with eunuchs— sexually non-normative people.

This is the story: Jesus was healing when he was interrupted by the legal specialists who wanted to ask a trick question. "Is it lawful for a man to divorce his wife for any and every reason?" Quoting Moses from two sources, Gen 1:27 and 2:24, Jesus asked them, "Haven't you read that at the beginning the Creator 'made them male and female,' and said 'for this reason a man will leave his father and mother and be united to his wife, and the two will become one flesh?' So they are no longer two, but one. Therefore what God has joined together, let man not separate." The Pharisees challenged Jesus again: "Then why did Moses command that a man give his wife a certificate of divorce and send her away?" In his reply, Jesus seemed to expose their attitude: "Moses permitted you to divorce your wives because your hearts were hard. But it was not this way from the beginning." What Jesus did was extraordinary for a rabbi; he gave preference to one passage of Scripture over another. To Jesus, the passages in Genesis had priority over the later laws of Moses.

One disciple, perhaps betraying his own hard heart, exclaimed, "If this is the situation between a husband and wife, it is better not to marry!" Seeming to take him at his word, Jesus then made his pronouncement about eunuchs. He said, "Not everyone can accept this teaching, but only those to whom it is given. For there are eunuchs who have been so from birth, and there are eunuchs who have been made eunuchs by others, and there are eunuchs who have made themselves eunuchs for the sake of the kingdom of heaven. Let anyone accept this who can." I struggled to understand what eunuchs had to do with the topic of marriage and divorce, but in my struggle, I did not fail to notice that Jesus asserted twice that his point about eunuchs might be challenging. I began to conclude that Jesus was making a larger point by contrasting two groups of people. People in the first group, because they were heterosexual, were privileged to enter into marriage and, as a concession, might divorce. People in the second group were those who, like eunuchs, were non-normative and could not share their privilege. He described three types of eunuchs: men who were "born that way," men who were "made that way" (I suspect by violence), and men who felt called to be celibate, whom he called "eunuchs for the sake of the kingdom." I was struck by the fact that Jesus made it clear that choice was a factor in only one type of eunuch. Having land and children was deemed the fruit of God's covenant with Israel, so for most Jewish men, to be a eunuch was unthinkable; it was practically a denial of God's covenant with Israel. So it must have been startling to them to be compared with eunuchs.

My new reading suggested to me that our modern understanding of the word "eunuch" does not do full justice to all who could be included within its meaning. In this context, eunuchs represent all sexually non-normative people, including gay men, lesbians, so-called "barren" women, people whose gender identity does not fit the male/female binary, and any other sexually non-normative group excluded from privilege.

I believe it was to remedy their hard hearts that Jesus urged these privileged men to think about eunuchs—sexually non-conforming men who were not at all like them. By contrasting them, he was pointing out that not everyone shared their hard hearts—hearts exposed by their heteronormative male privilege and their harsh perspective on the treatment of women. When I realized that Jesus pointed to our community as an example to remedy their hard hearts, I was amazed.

Of the thousands of people baptized into Jesus, most remain unknown to us, but it seems so precious to me that a sexually non-normative person, the Ethiopian Eunuch (Acts 8) receives special mention as perhaps the first Gentile convert.

When I came to appreciate that Jesus himself did not present as heteronormative, I was in awe. Jesus, as an unmarried rabbi, was the most significant of all non-normative people. I believe he affirms us by being like us in a unique way. When I finally came to believe that Jesus stands in solidarity with all of us by being like us, I felt like a prisoner set free. By relinquishing privilege, by choosing to be a "eunuch for the kingdom," I believe Christ elevates those of us who are non-normative, embracing us who once were excluded. It is as though Jesus assures us, "Be not ashamed, for I am with you."

11

And God Said: My Bad

S. R. Davis

My God, my God, why have you forsaken me?

—Matt 27:46

I felt like there had been a mistake for as long as I can remember. Everyone saw a girl, tried to make me dress and act like a girl, and my body mostly looked like a girl's. But I knew everyone and everything was wrong. I wore the costume and tried and still got tormented for never getting it right. I always got told I wouldn't be a real girl unless I started acting and looking different. They may as well have said that unless I started growing tentacles and soon, I'd never be a real cuttlefish. (Though I am an admirer, I never felt the need to wear a pair myself.) I could never be anything but a girl, they told me, and yet they constantly complained that I was failing to be one.

I thought that if I believed in God, I had to believe that God doesn't make mistakes and that everything happens for a reason. I imagined elaborate explanations: maybe I was a terrible man in a past life, some baby-raping monster put into a woman's body this go-round for my own and others' protection. Maybe I was the reincarnation of some alt-right pick-up artist plunged into this purgatory to learn a lesson. Maybe my soul had previously been in a gay man in some repressive regime who prayed for this compromise so he could love a man in safety.

Yet, what type of God would play such snarky games? None I could believe in. But that still left me with this conundrum: Was I wrong or did God make mistakes?

I've often wondered if maybe Jesus didn't die *for* our sins but rather *because* of our sins. Obviously, executing a man because he's annoying, or heretical, or simply because you can is pretty sinful—sin certainly caused Jesus's death. But what if Jesus died not just because the crowd, the religious leaders, or the corrupt government demanded it but because we, now, demand it?

Let's say Jesus comes to earth, instead, as a king, who could say whatever he wants. Or even if he merely comes to a nicer, gentler part of earth: he proclaims on Haight and Ashbury that he's the Son of God and hippies say, "Right on!" and some say he doesn't put on as good a show as Edwin, the Son of God who doesn't just heal girls but cuts them in half first, and the suits scream, "Get a job!" and he is mostly tolerated and he dies peacefully of old age. Wouldn't that be good enough?

My Jewish mother taught me a wonderful song for Passover— "If He had brought us out of Egypt, *Dayenu*," "If He had split the sea for us, *Dayenu*"—that would have been enough, fifteen stanzas of interventions by God that each would be sufficient reason to worship. If God had come to earth a hippy, *Dayenu*?

It wouldn't be enough for me because of my sins. I'm a miserable, petty thing who, if I got to meet God incarnated as King Jesus or Hippy Jesus, would probably say, "Yeah, but do you really know what it's like to be human?" I am forever uncertain if there's a God who hears my prayers, or if there's a divine purpose, or if my life matters—and those uncertainties cause me pain. Maybe those painful uncertainties are part of what being human is. I'm not sure King Jesus or Hippy Jesus would know that pain.

And this is why I demand Jesus dies a senseless, torturous death. Because the God who I can understand understanding me knows what it's like to say, "My God, why have you forsaken me?" Like an angry teenager yelling at their parents, given the chance to give God a piece of my mind, I'd scream, "I didn't ask to be born! You don't know what it's like!" God on the cross, abandoned, dying a miserable, meaningless death leaves me gobsmacked.

Does God make mistakes? I'm beginning to think so. Certainly, everything's not perfect. There is suffering. Our fragile little selves are in fragile little bodies. The same sinful self that demands that Jesus has to die sometimes gets so angry at this messed up world that it wants to see a do-over. Like Jonah, like Lot's wife, I want to watch it burn. That's why I like that horror story we recount in Precious Moments figurines and baby onesies. There's a flood because I know the world is messed up with even more certainty than I know there's an omnipotent God who could plow it under. And I know that if it were in my power, I probably would turn on the taps the first time someone cut me off in traffic or called me "Ma'am." Because of my sins, I need the stories of the flood and Jesus's crucifixion to accept that God is aware that creation isn't perfect, but loves it anyway. I don't really think God did a do-over, just that God created a world with tectonic plates, gravity, rain, and expiry-dated life-forms—life-forms which could eventually look at cataracts and glacial erratics and say, "Whoa! Somebody must have really made God angry!"

"The Lord said in his heart 'I will never again curse the ground because of humankind, for the inclination of the human heart is evil from youth; nor will I ever again destroy every living creature as I have done'" (Gen 8:21). This assures me that there can be a God even if there's been some mistake matching this soul to this body. Somehow there's a glitch in the mechanisms that knit together my DNA, mechanisms that boggle my mind how orderly they actually do work, even given that all of us have some glitches in there. It's glitches that occasionally, but continually, give rise to new creation.

The crucifixion tells me God is intimately aware of the sinfulness of creatures, the same creatures who think up a story about how they'd slash and burn it if they could, and still, God maintains and lives in this imperfect creation.

Maybe God is perfect—but perfect needs nothing. Perfect is so done, so sealed off, and finished. Perfect is lifeless. It's my imperfectness that makes me need the God who can say, "My bad." Maybe it is in the glitches and imperfections that God lives.

12

Magnificat: Seriously, God?

JENNIFER HASLER

My soul greatly magnifies the Lord, And my spirit rejoices in the God who saved me, For he (God) looked upon the humiliation of his female slave. From now on, all generations will call me blessed. . . .

—LUKE 1:46–48 (INTERPRETED BY JENNIFER HASLER)

Let us go back a month or two earlier as Mary begins just another day. She is starting to make loaves of bread in the small brick home built into the Nazareth hills. She is looking forward to life with her husband-to-be, Joseph, just outside the growing town of Sepphoris.

Then, an Angel appears. Not just any angel, but the angel Gabriel, the same angel that visited Zechariah months ago. And this is not the holy of holies. What an interruption!

A baby? Really? You know, I was not looking to have a child yet. I've never done anything. . . . Oh, God will do this to me through the Holy Spirit. OK, who am I to oppose God? Joseph won't be happy. The village won't be happy.

Mary handles the announcement better than Zechariah, but it will bring humiliation, this something that God will do to her. Mary remembers stories of what happened to unmarried women who were pregnant: stoned, run out of town. There are many ways not to live.

Mary travels far away to see her Cousin Elizabeth. She remembered the angel said something about Elizabeth. She travels alone (*women don't travel alone*) from Galilee to Judea, fighting morning sickness. Women don't travel when pregnant (*they are kept hidden away*).

The two children in their mothers' wombs recognize each other! Mary begins to be excited at what is about to happen, yet still remembering, still afraid.

> My soul greatly magnifies the Lord,
> And my spirit rejoices in the God who saved me,
> For he (God) looked upon the humiliation of his female slave.
> From now on, all generations will call me blessed. . . .

Mary has come to understand that God made her for this purpose. She begins to understand that being transparent about what God did to her—that she is pregnant with God's child—and will do, frees her so she will become prophetic, as illustrated by the next verses.

It takes Mary time to be at peace with what God called her to do. Her journey back to Galilee three months later brings up the old fears. She knows she would have to face everyone in town, including Joseph. She is showing. *No one will understand. No one will believe how I got pregnant.*

What would you do? For some, this is not theory.

I connected the story of Mary to the transgender experience when God called me to come out as transgender while hearing an advent sermon in the Bay Area. I could feel both God and the very center of my being calling me to come out yet, like Mary, feeling disturbed, fearful, terrified, and uncertain. Mary's story seemed to mimic my story.

This was before transition. Before transition I was married, with two kids, and had a successful career. One could find a hundred others who would face a similar situation, so my background was not unusual. Many of them would result in terrible ends, losing their kids, losing their career, being homeless, working in prostitution. Any surprise that forty-six percent of transgender people attempt suicide?

Seriously God, you want me to do what?

Like Mary, it took time. I remember a year later finally emerging out into the world at a Christmas party. Although I was over thirty years old at that point, the girl inside was maybe at thirteen year old maturity, like Mary, like many who come out. I remember getting out of the car, with others, my feet touching the ground, feeling the freedom as well as the terror immigrating to this new, yet familiar world.

I transitioned publicly in church, first at Menlo Park Presbyterian Church in San Francisco and then in my home United Methodist Church in Atlanta, Georgia. I found a depth of connection to God unlike I had ever known. My faith has since been about authentically trusting and walking with God; it is not just an intellectual pursuit. Being in church was emotional throughout my journey, often just simply looking at the cross and pouring out my heart: "Thank you, thank you, thank you." When I was at my first chapel service at Candler School of Theology, I almost could not believe where God had brought me, and yet, I knew I was exactly in the right place.

One day early in my transition, someone from the trans community approached me to ask about the cross around my neck. "Are you Christian?" "Yes," I responded. Five minutes later, the same person asked, after others had moved away, "no, really. Are you a practicing Christian?" "Actually, yes," I said. The questioner then asked, shocked and amazed, "How is that possible?" She gave me an opportunity to explain how faith empowers transition rather than fighting against it. The hands and feet of Christ could enter a space that few could have entered because few could relate to these situations.

Several in the trans community, struggling between authenticity and faith, would experience the almost unbelievable possibility: they could be authentic and have a relationship with God. Some never thought they would survive the experience, but they flourished. I am so thankful for the journey God led me on, following the inspiration of Mary's story of becoming authentic. One can only truly express one's prophetic voice, even in the retelling of this story, when one is truly authentic.

As I experienced it, Mary's story was not just a nice tale told at Christmas with everything sanitized so as not to offend the hearers. No. One can hear the depth of the prayer of acceptance both in Mary's day and even in my personal experience:

> My soul greatly magnifies the Lord,
> And my spirit rejoices in the God who saved me,
> For he (God) looked upon the humiliation of his female slave.

Praise be to God!

13

My Great Hunger

KENNY PIERCE

About noon the next day, as they were on their journey and approaching the city, Peter went up on the roof to pray. He became hungry and wanted something to eat; and while it was being prepared, he fell into a trance. He saw the heaven opened and something like a large sheet coming down, being lowered to the ground by its four corners. In it were all kinds of four-footed creatures and reptiles and birds of the air. Then he heard a voice saying, "Get up, Peter; kill and eat." But Peter said, "By no means, Lord; for I have never eaten anything that is profane or unclean." The voice said to him again, a second time, "What God has made clean, you must not call profane." This happened three times, and the thing was suddenly taken up to heaven.

—ACTS 10:9–16

It was the summer of 1985. I was at a parish retreat just before my twenty-first birthday. Our priest spoke eloquently to those sitting in their metal chairs hanging on his every word. I'd grown up sitting in those chairs, but that day my job was to serve food to these, God's sanctified, and I did so dutifully.

I'd worked at retreats before, but this one was different. Something had shifted in me the year prior to this retreat, a realization that I was "something different" and that "something" had a name. I was no longer the same altar boy that these people thought they knew so well.

The topic for the session that day was "Reconciliation With the Prodigal." The priest intoned: "Mother church stands ready to accept the fallen, the prodigal back into their fold. Whether theirs is the sin of adultery, fornication, pedophilia, murder, theft, homosexuality, masturbation, we stand ready to welcome back the prodigal." The hall was silent and disapproving as our priest uttered this conditional nod to the unclean. Finally, a woman who'd known me since infancy retorted: "The Bible is clear that homosexuality is among the greatest mortal sins, and there's no way I'll accept those people. Ever."

In that instant, I understood my new place among the outcasts on the other side of the doors of those banquet halls and chapels. Instead of the sacred communion host, a bitter choice was laid upon my tongue. I either could "not act upon my sin" and conform by marrying or joining the priesthood, or I could pursue my "lifestyle" and be relegated to Hell for all of eternity.

That was no choice. The voice that I assumed was God had always told me that I was never alone and had commanded me to be true to who I was. Now, I wondered if that voice were actually that of the Satan. I stopped listening. I stopped believing. And so it was that my Great Hunger for a community began.

In the early days of my Hunger, I ran from place to place, looking for food and drink, as they, the chosen, grew fat inside, engorging themselves on the feast that overflowed their gilded tables. There was every delicacy imaginable for God's chosen. I could never hope to be seated at their banquet table. On occasion, I'd look through the windows to see if perhaps I might slip in somehow, but the authentic me was clearly unwelcome behind those massive gilded doors made of walnut and wrought iron, manned by God's valiant soldiers.

Kill that part of you, and then you may eat. At first I tried to obey. *Kill, then eat.* Many of us tried to kill the profane beast within. But how? Prayer wouldn't work—I couldn't pray my spirit to death, try though I might.

Perhaps the wine that we'd enjoyed at communion would drown the unclean within me. I drank glass after glass in those early years of the Hunger, enough to blind me to myself. A little went far at first, but before long four glasses began to feel more like four sips. This was a powerful beast that held sway over my spirit. It would demand something stronger. Tanqueray and tonic, Long Island iced teas, vodka martinis, pitcher after pitcher of beer flowed unabated until I grew blind to my filth and could forget—if only for a few hours.

But the filthy beast, dead within me night after night, would rise like a phoenix from my ashes at dawn. It was a powerful thing, this abomination within me that refused to die, and month after month, year after year, I grew hungrier for all that I lost, all that was forbidden to those like me.

In this time of my Great Hunger, the feast mattered little to our lesioned and emaciated brothers and sisters dying in great numbers from AIDS. We all starved then. We starved for compassion, for mercy, for advocacy, for kindness from those who dined and laughed and congratulated one another on their purity. The hunger pangs were not as severe during those hours spent at benefits, selling tickets, or volunteering at hospices. I survived as those years passed, largely by the grace and support of another community, another kind of holiness and, in 1997, the dying began to abate, some sixteen years after it began.

And then, in 1999, I finally succumbed to the alcohol that never assuaged my inner thirst, and my body began to fail me. I awoke in rehab one January morning, with my Great Hunger roaring like a beast still within me, in all of its unbridled fury. I wished for some reprieve from this Hell, and death by my own hand was a seductive suitor.

On the first night of detox, between tremors and vomiting as I tossed and turned in a bed of my own fevered sweat, I could have sworn that I heard a familiar voice within me once more. I chalked it up to the hallucinations of withdrawal, but its cadence is as clear to me now as it was eighteen years ago: *You have never been alone. You were never unclean. And you were never meant to be hungry. I am still here. Now kill and eat, Kenny.*

It took years to find my way to a banquet of Christian community again. Trust came slowly, largely at the behest of other Christians who also had been cast out of their communities. There was the woman, aching to be a pastor to her people, who was told that her gender made her unfit for the calling. There was the sexual abuse survivor who said that her short skirt brought on those "justifiable advances." There was the man who was told that his beloved gay cousin, the one who had died by his own hand when his church and family shut him out, was now burning in his rightful place in Hell. There was the homeless man who was told that his sleeping that cold winter at the doors of the church was making the congregants uncomfortable and sullying the sidewalk, and that he would have to leave. They were now experiencing their Great Hunger as well and had nowhere to turn out in the wilderness but to one another.

We stumbled onto one another over time by happenstance or God's hand. Over time we have become slayers together, killers of false voices within us that would have us believe the messages deeming us filthy and unworthy to sit at God's holy table.

The essential work of killing those voices within has never been easy. In letting go, in surrendering ourselves to communal holiness, I have learned what it really means to die to myself, and to be resurrected in community from the margins. Some three decades after I was first named unclean, the false voices are gone and my Great Hunger has died with them.

14

Prince Charming

TODD McGRAW

Love is patient; love is kind; love is not envious or boastful or arrogant
or rude. It does not insist on its own way; it is not irritable or resentful;
it does not rejoice in wrongdoing, but rejoices in the truth. It bears all
things, believes all things, hopes all things, endures all things.

—1 COR 13:4–7

A peach blue sky was overhead on a beautiful Friday evening.
I felt the sand between my toes as I came across it: "Love
is patient, love is kind. . . ." I felt the tears stream down my face,
but my soul beamed with bliss. I had the answers for which I had
been looking. These profound words provided me with the inner
peace, calmness, stillness, and self-love that I had been seeking for
twenty-three years.

Being gay, I've always had a hard time believing that God,
or really anyone, could fully love me. Growing up in a rural West
Virginia town, I was surrounded perpetually by a community that
failed to accept anything that was a deviation from the perceived

perfect "Christian" life. I knew I was an anomaly. I didn't know what love was, where to find it, how to give it, or how to receive it. You may ask: how did I not know what love was? The truth is I didn't know I was worthy enough to be loved or to give love.

"Love is patient; love is kind" was a game changer. After reading it for the first time, my soul radiated with love—self-love. Love finally made sense. I started to get it. I knew that God loved me. I understood that if you don't know God loves you that to love yourself is impossible. I knew this because I understood that love starts with knowing God loves you, loving yourself. Then these two one-of-a-kind loves emancipate your soul so it has the capacity to love others. I knew that the love I yearned to give to another young man one day was okay; I knew that being gay was okay.

This Scripture taught me that love is patient—that there is no timeline on love, that God will bring your self-acceptance and your soulmate to you in God's timing, not yours. Love is kind. The love we yearn to give another soul is good-natured.

Love does not provoke jealousy. Nor does it suggest that I should be with a female because I am jealous of the "normal lifestyle" or that I should have to fancy a beard for my ego.

Love is not dishonest. If I were to try to be with a female, that would be the most dishonest thing I could ever do—to pretend to love another soul because society said I should. Love is not about trying to raise my status in society—rather it is about how my soul will dance every day once I meet my soulmate.

Love does not produce displeasure or hostility at a female because I know that my soul will never leap with happiness to spend the rest of my life with her.

Love is forgiving. No matter how many times we go astray or give less than our best to God, God already has forgiven us, and we should do the same with our soulmate. The love God has for us supersedes any lie we have ever lived, including myself living a lie about who I am for twenty-three years.

Love does not build itself on a lie—the lie that I was attracted to females. Love does not succumb to the evils of heteronormativity but love rejoices in the truth—that I am attracted to males, gay males.

I understood that love always protects the truth—that I am attracted to gay men who have had the courage to be their whole-hearted selves. Love always trusts in the God who made me not in humankind, which wants me to be someone else. Love always trusts that God will help me to persevere through the hardships that face so many of us LGBTQ folks. These hardships which began for me in rural West Virginia when I thought that my voice was too high-pitched, my traits too feminine, my clothes too neat for people who saw me only as a gay boy and not as a future youth pastor. I understood the truth that being gay was a beautiful gift with which God blessed me.

Love hopes. I hope that one day I will find love with my Prince Charming. Our love will inspire others who are yearning for the love God created them to have.

This love hopes that every little gay boy, little gay girl, and little transgender boy or girl will have the opportunity to live as their wholehearted selves without receiving criminal punishment from the seventy-seven countries where homosexuality is illegal and the five countries where being gay is punishable by death. This love hopes that little bisexual girl or boy will empty out the bottle of pain pills and fill up the bottle with self-love and that they will then give it abundantly to the boy or girl God created them to spend the rest of their life with.

I believe that love always perseveres. No matter what anyone says, does, or thinks—the love I will have one day with my Prince Charming, the love you will have with your Prince Charming or Princess Charming—will overcome any obstacle that the enemy throws our way because true love always perseveres.[1]

---

1. Thanks to Cheryl Carithers at the Texas Christian University Writing Center for proofreading this essay.

15

Love Letter

Stephen V. Sprinkle

Beloved, let us love one another because love is of God;
everyone who loves is born of God and knows God.

—1 John 4:7

God is love. Long after the writer of 1 John penned these words, I encountered the message that opened my heart. That message of divine love broke into the fortress of my soul, outflanked my anxieties, and salved my bruised self-esteem. As a gay teenager in the North Carolina foothills, no gay role models or LGBTQ community were available to me. I was an isolated kid, cheerful on the outside, but secretly torn between an attraction for my own gender and the anti-gay messages aimed at such feelings, ingrained in the evangelical culture of my birth. With God's Love Letter, the Holy Spirit infiltrated my closeted, hyper-guarded soul, and midwifed a new consciousness within me.

I cannot overestimate the influence 1 John had upon me. I was reared in a rural church where the Bible was revered—and though I never heard attacks against queer folk in any service there, anti-gay bias grew like weeds along the country roads of my school district. Public school crackled with the usual, furtive locker room explorations of young bodies as well as the raw terror of being labeled "one of them" by peers and adults. Into that morass of emotions, the message that "God is love" challenged my internal conflicts about myself, about what decency means, and about my place in the world of relationships.

"Little children, let us love, not in word or speech, but in truth and action." Sacred love, 1 John taught, was not just an idea. It was enacted in the real world, between real, embodied people! As I read how anxiety was powerless to overcome the bedrock truth of love, my confidence increased: "And by this we will know that we are from the truth and will reassure our hearts before [God] whenever our hearts condemn us; for God is greater than our hearts, and [God] knows everything."

Only the Bible itself could have convinced me of the holy origins of my same-sex yearnings in those days. Authority figures throughout my culture held that homosexuality was "against the Bible." They marshaled cherry-picked passages from Genesis, Leviticus, and Romans to purge the faithful of "unclean" desires. A biblical knot, you see, could only be untangled by reasoning text against text. First John taught me with its beautiful simplicity that God's Spirit filled and made sense of the Bible, and was not wrathful, legalistic, or judgmental. No, instead, the works and ways of the mysterious Creator-God were *Christ-like*, the most significant theological insight I gained in all of my teenage years: "No one has ever seen God; if we love one another, God lives in us and [God's] love is perfected in us."

Ah! The love of God is a queer thing! God, the genesis of all that is, gave rise to same-gender affection and fidelity as acts of divine, Christ-like love, right alongside all other expressions of genuine human commitment. Though I did not yet know the words "sensual" and "erotic," I began to understand that the practice of love, truly divine love, took place in the exchange of affection all people had with one another—LGBTQ people, too.

Over time, the writer of 1 John helped dispel my fears. It lent me enough courage to embrace the incarnate image and likeness of

God on display in myself and the people around me: "There is no fear in love, but perfect love casts out fear; for fear has to do with punishment and whoever fears has not reached perfection in love."

My parochialism took a beating in the years that followed. Practical lessons of Christlike love never come easily! Jesus Christ is indeed the Way for me, but I see now that many paths lead to human flourishing. I have also learned that in the matters of love, I am an eternal novice. Wisdom comes the hard way with many missteps—often, sadly, the same ones, time and again. I have failed many times in my spiritual life and in my relationships. I have hurt others and been hurt, while I continue to relearn the lessons of mutual forgiveness. Such, I have come to understand, is the way love comes closer to the authenticity taught in 1 John—and to joy!

Thankfully, I now perceive a richer Christlikeness that celebrates all manner of differences and doctrines for all sorts and conditions of people—some who embrace a faith and those who are faith-free. Justice and mercy are the closest companions of the incarnate love manifest in all systems and sects of humanity. Divine love breaks down barriers through the effects of its steadfast, self-evident truths: "Those who say, 'I love God,' and hate their brothers and sisters, are liars; for those who do not love a brother or a sister whom they have seen, cannot love God whom they have not seen."

Though I was ordained to the ministry thirty-nine years ago, I continually encounter how faulty my understandings are—how partial and fragmentary, as John's co-theologian Paul once wrote, "Now I know only in part; then I will know fully, even as I have been fully known" (1 Cor 13:12). Scholars may propose many likely reasons John wrote the first letter to his first century community, yet for me, it has always been personal. John wrote the clearest love letter in the New Testament, and beyond any intention he could have had at the time, its message set me free to live out my queerness beyond my fears and to work for a better world. Long after the initial reasons John penned his little book have been buried in obscurity, its central insistence that God is love continues to attract us to it, beckoning us to open up our closets and come out into the light.

16

Falling in Love

RAY JORDAN

Beloved, let us love one another, because love is from God;
everyone who loves is born of God and knows God.
Whoever does not love does not know God, for God is love.

—1 JOHN 4:7–8

I am the Alpha and the Omega, the first and the last,
the beginning and the end.

—REV 22:13

Yes, God is love. God is not like love or similar to love, nor do God and love have a few things in common. Rather, God is love. The two are synonymous. Though it sounds simple, this was the revelation I gained after a year of intensely studying love and teaching a Bible study on the subjects of faith, love, and healing. I had so ingrained this idea into my mind and heart that the inseparability of God and the essence of love had become a part of my daily reality. Therefore, when I fell in love with a man, my life would forever change.

Did I forget to mention that I am also male? Yes, I am a man who fell in love with another man. By twenty-first century standards this may seem like a simple and non-newsworthy notion; however, for years my sexual struggle was a dirty little secret. It was a secret I muttered to no one. In fact, the words "I am gay" were so unfathomable I wouldn't speak them aloud to myself nor would I even dare to pray about the possibility. Just ponder that for a moment. I was so filled with shame and self-loathing that I was an adult before I could even pray about it and, by then, my prayers were only desperate pleas to be changed and to be somehow different.

This was the vicious cycle that engulfed my teen and young adult years. In part, I was so afraid to be me, I was in a never-ending rat race, a disorienting maze, a house of horrors—that is until the Word of God set me free. Yes, but the Word of God is not to be confused with the Bible. "For the letter kills, but the Spirit gives life" (2 Cor 3:6b). However, the Word of God is the life-giving, God-breathed inspiration that only Spirit can lift from the pages of Scripture and offer as a healing balm. Yes, it was this revelation that set me free!

I had been taught, no doubt through a toxic theology, that being gay was the result of a "lust spirit," a demon even. Therefore, if I fought valiantly, through spiritual warfare of some kind, I could exorcise myself of the problem. However, at the age of twenty-five, when I met and fell in love with a man, I had to confront and eventually defeat that toxic theology. But isn't that the cure for all toxic theology—a healthy dose of love?

My yearlong study of love and God and the love of God had thoroughly persuaded me that God is love. Furthermore, I was convinced that since God is love that anywhere God is, love must be present; anywhere love is, God must be in the midst. Therefore, it is God who enables or gives us the ability to have and to express love. So, when I found myself in real, true, life-giving love with another man I became confused as to why God would give me the ability to love him. Similarly, if I loved him, did that mean God was present, because God is love, right?

This experience was the epitome of epiphany. Again, it's so simple but it was a real "aha" moment for me. Being gay was not about with whom one has sex, being gay is about whom you Love! Being gay is about with whom you have the emotional capacity to love and experience intimacy, and a romantic or sexual relationship is just an extension of that intimacy.

This was particularly true of the person with whom I had fallen in love. He and I lived in different states, therefore physical intimacy was not the key component of our relationship; love was. We didn't see each other enough to have an extensive sexual relationship, but I sure loved him. I genuinely, honestly, sincerely, passionately, unselfishly "1 Corinthians 13" loved him. I was liberated at the very thought! One could almost hear the shackles of shame and guilt fall from my mind and heart.

The rest is history. My life would never be the same, nor would my theology. While it took me another eight years to come to grips with my faith and my relationship with the Divine, one thing never left me, that is the revelation of God and the inseparability of the Holy and the essence and presence of Love. Still today, when I see the word "God" in the Scriptures, I often replace it with the word "Love" because God equals Love. So, if God is the Alpha and the Omega, guess what? Love is the Alpha and the Omega. Yes, simply stated: Love is the beginning and it is the end. At least in the story of my journey, no words are more true.

Conclusion

E arlier I asked, "What do LGBTQ Christians bring to the task of biblical interpretation?" My answer—a sense of redemptive purpose, as these essays, poems, and remembrances show. My prayer is that this little volume will find its way into the hands of other LGBTQ Christians struggling with the tension between who they are and what too many Christians have told them they should be, that it falls into the hands of LGBTQ Christians' parents, and that it falls into the hands of church leaders who need to hear that the ones they have condemned may become the ones who rescue the relevance of the Bible in Christians' lives, rescue the church, and perhaps, rescue the God in whose image lesbians, gays, bisexual, transgender, genderqueer, and all the other queer people were made. Amen.

Ellin Sterne Jimmerson

Glossary

Bisexual: one with a sexual attraction to both males and females

Cisgender: one whose identity and body matches the gender they were assigned at birth

Clobber passages: passages or verses in the Bible often interpreted to condemn homosexuality and used to "clobber" LGBTQ people

Gay: a man who is sexually attracted only to other men; an umbrella term for lesbians, gays, bisexual, transgender, and genderqueer people

Genderqueer: one whose gender is neither male nor female or is both male and female; one whose gender is ambiguous

Lesbian: a woman who is sexually attracted only to other women

Queer: a slur for anyone who is not a heterosexual male or female; one who is unique in matters relating to gender and/or sexuality; a lesbian, gay man, bisexual, transgender, or other person who is not a heterosexual male or female; a rejection of gender and sexual identity

Queerness: non-normativity; uniqueness in matters relating to gender and/or sexuality; existential uniqueness

Heteronormativity: relating to the idea that heterosexuality is the ideal or normal state of sexual attraction

Heterosexuality: sexual attraction to members of the opposite sex

Homosexuality: sexual attraction to members of the same sex

Normative: an ideal standard for that which is considered normal

Normativity: relating to an ideal standard for that which is considered normal

Transgender: people whose outward gender identity, i.e., male or female, does not match their inward gender identity, for example a male in a female body or a female in a male body

Contributors

Ellin Sterne Jimmerson, editor, holds a Master of Arts in US History from Samford University, a Master of Theological Studies with a concentration in Latin American liberation theology from Vanderbilt Divinity School, and a PhD in US History from the University of Houston. Her specialization is the intersection of politics and Christianity. She wrote and directed the award winning migrant advocacy documentary, *The Second Cooler*, narrated by Martin Sheen. An ordained Baptist minister, Jimmerson gained international attention when she officiated at the first same sex wedding in Madison County, Alabama. Following the wedding, she resigned her position as minister to the community at her home church in Huntsville, Alabama, which subsequently was disfellowshipped by the Southern Baptist Convention. She is the author of numerous articles on issues surrounding both immigration and LGBTQ people. You can follow her on Facebook (Rev. Dr. Ellin Jimmerson) and her blog at ellinjimmersonblog.wordpress.com and find out more about *The Second Cooler* at www.thesecondcooler.com.

Richard Barham was reared in Bridgeport, Alabama. He started preaching on a regular basis at age fifteen. He graduated from the University of Alabama (Tuscaloosa) with a Bachelor of Arts in history and a minor in religious studies. He attended the New Orleans Baptist Theological Seminary. Before coming out, he served as an interim pastor at First Baptist Church of Bridgeport, Alabama, and as pastor of Kennedy Baptist Church in Kennedy, Alabama. After coming out, Barham served as the associate pastor at Covenant Community Church in Birmingham. Since December, 1999, he has served as the senior pastor of Spirit of the Cross Church in Huntsville, Alabama. He has volunteered for various community LGBTQ organizations and has served on the board of directors of the AIDS Action Coalition of Huntsville (now Thrive Alabama), Soulforce Alabama, and GLBT Advocacy and Youth Services (now Free2Be). He is a frequent guest on local college panels and local media regarding gay and religious issues.

Riley Chattin is a spiritual director in Roanoke, Virginia. He is a self-professed seeker of truth in Christianity. It was in gender transition that he experienced the undeniable connection to God that he believes we all share.

S. R. Davis is genderqueer. She teaches high school students with developmental disabilities. She has a Bachelor of Arts in English and Philosophy and a Master of Arts in English from McMaster University, a Bachelor of Education from York University, and studied theology at Emmanuel College of the University of Toronto. She is passionate about disability rights, opera, and the novels of Marilynne Robinson. She lives with her partner, one-year-old daughter, and a retired racing greyhound named Lady Gaga in Toronto, Canada. Please contact her @SRLimDavis.

Lisa A. Dordal holds a Master of Divinity and a Master of Fine Arts, both from Vanderbilt University, and currently teaches in the English Department at Vanderbilt. She is a Pushcart Prize nominee and the recipient of an Academy of American Poets Prize and the Robert Watson Poetry Prize. Her poetry has appeared in a variety of journals including *Best New Poets, Cave Wall, CALYX, The Greensboro Review, Vinyl Poetry*, and *The Journal of Feminist Studies in Religion*. Her first full-length collection of poetry, *Mosaic of the Dark*, is forthcoming from Black Lawrence Press (2018). She lives in Nashville, Tennessee. For more information about her poetry or to be added to her mailing list, please visit her website at lisadordal.com.

Andrew Dykstra was born in the city of Bolsward in the province of Friesland in the Netherlands. With his parents and his sister, Sofie, Dykstra immigrated to Canada in 1952. He was raised in the Reformed Church in America (RCA) but at age twenty-two became a member of the Seventh-day Adventist Church. Feeling that there was no home for him there as a gay man, Dykstra eventually withdrew for twenty years but returned in 2000. He retired from the printing business in 2016 after working in various capacities for forty-seven years. He currently lives in Toronto, Ontario, Canada where he is an active member of Immanuel Seventh-day Adventist Church. He can be contacted at adykstra@teksavvy.com.

Jonathan Freeman-Coppadge is a writer and a new father. He is the fiction editor at *Oyster River Pages*, and he teaches English at Groton School where he lives with his husband and their son. You can find him on Medium and Twitter @jdcoppadge.

Jennifer Hasler is a part-time theology student at Candler School of Theology at Emory University in Atlanta, Georgia. She is a full professor in Electrical and Computer Engineering at the Georgia Institute of Technology. She transitioned from male to female between 2006 and 2012, keeping both her academic position, and more importantly, her family together. Hasler has been married for twenty-one years and has two children, ages seventeen and fourteen. Her entry was written to commemorate the eighteenth Transgender Day of Remembrance, a solemn day in the transgender community which remembers those who were murdered during the previous year. She particularly wanted to remember Gwen Araujo, a Fremont, California, trans woman who was killed by four men after forcibly finding out she was transgender.

Jeff Hood holds a Master of Arts, a Master of Science, a Master of Divinity, a Master of Theology, and a Doctor of Ministry. He is an activist theologian and author of fifteen books and numerous articles. In 2013, Hood was awarded PFLAG, Fort Worth's Equality Award for activism and service. In 2016, Hood's book, *The Courage to Be Queer*, was named the third best religion book of the year at the Independent Publishers Book Awards. Through consistent media appearances, Hood has been able to share the message of queerness with a broad audience. He lives in Denton, Texas.

Ray Jordan currently serves as the interim senior pastor of Central Congregational United Church of Christ of Dallas, Texas, after serving as Central's associate pastor. He has also worked in the public and private sectors as a public school teacher, university professor, nonprofit administrator, corporate trainer, and consultant. Although originally from Oakland, California, Jordan was raised by his grandmother on a farm in rural Arkansas, where he often traversed the intersectionality of his race (African American), class (poor), and sexuality (gay). He holds a Bachelor of Science in Health Education, a Master of Arts in Teaching, a Master of Theological Studies from Southern Methodist University's Perkins School of Theology, and is completing his PhD (ABD) from Union Institute and University. In addition to pastoring, Jordan serves on the board of directors of the South Central Conference of the United Church of Christ, teaches classes in interdisciplinary studies and African American studies at the University of Texas at Arlington, teaches classes in political science at Southern Methodist University, and spends time with his three children—Trey, Alley, and Joshua Caleb.

Tyler Heston is a second-year Master of Divinity student at Brite Divinity School and serves as the assistant minister for middle school at University Christian Church in Fort Worth, Texas. He graduated with a degree in religion in society and a certificate in nonprofit management from the University of Memphis. Raised in a nondenominational evangelical church in suburban Memphis, Tennessee, Tyler joined Kingsway Christian Church (Disciples of Christ) after coming out as gay while he was in college and now serves as a council member for the GLAD Alliance, which works toward "transforming the Christian Church (Disciples of Christ) into a just and inclusive church that welcomes persons of all gender expressions and sexual identities into the full life and leadership of the church." Aside from school and ministry, he enjoys a variety of things, such as Sufjan Stevens's music, *The X-Files*, traveling, and eating sushi with friends.

Todd McGraw grew up in rural West Virginia where his spiritual life was basically nonexistent. His family attended church because, like many other families in his community, they knew that to keep up with the Joneses, they had to pray with the Joneses. They attended church, but for him God and faith seemed distant and bleak. He was a young, gay male struggling to reconcile a religious teaching that shunned homosexuals with the reality that, in spite of all the bravado and gentility, he was gay and could do nothing to change it. He attended the University of Georgia on a swimming scholarship. After college, he accepted a lucrative corporate job in Atlanta. At twenty-three, God became the epicenter of his life. He left the corporate job to attend Brite Divinity School at Texas Christian University. A youth pastor at Preston Hollow Presbyterian Church, McGraw lives in Fort Worth, Texas.

Kenny Pierce, a native of Southern California, came out in 1985 as the AIDS epidemic raged around him in the Greater Los Angeles area and later during his years spent living in San Francisco. He is passionate about God and about the needs of the changing church. He is dedicated to building bridges to the survivors and their families and friends, alienated and disillusioned by the church's betrayal and silence during the "gay genocide" in those earliest years of HIV/AIDS in America. Pierce lives in Vancouver, British Columbia, Canada. You can follow him on Twitter (@KennyRayPierce) and on his blog, *Tangentials*.

Stephen V. Sprinkle is professor of practical theology at Brite Divinity School, located on the campus of Texas Christian University in Fort Worth, Texas, and has held the office of director of field education and supervised ministry since 1994. He is the first openly gay scholar in Brite's history. A native of North Carolina, he holds a Bachelor of Arts from Barton College, a Master of Divinity from Yale University Divinity School, and a PhD in Systematic Theology from Duke University. He is an ordained minister of the Alliance

79

of Baptists. Sprinkle was named 2010–2011 Hero of Hope by the Cathedral of Hope in Dallas for his advocacy on behalf of the LGBTQ community and served as Theologian in Residence for the cathedral for six years. In 2016, he received the Pillar of Freedom Award for his passion, activism, and dedication to the advancement of justice and human rights. He has authored three books and many scholarly articles and holds professional memberships in the Academy of Religious Leadership and the Association of Theological Field Educators. Sprinkle is a human rights advocate, a widely sought after speaker and pulpiteer, and an internationally recognized authority on anti-LGBTQ hate crimes.

Peterson Toscano uses storytelling to promote justice and equality. Through original performance lectures, Peterson opens up discussions about LGBTQ issues, privilege, the Bible, justice, and climate change. He created the performance lecture *Transfigurations—Transgressing Gender in the Bible*, which unearths gender non-conforming Bible characters. His personal essays about his experiences with conversion therapy have appeared in the Gay and Lesbian Review, Liturgy Magazine, and Huffington Post. He contributed to the Lambda Award winning anthology, *Gender Outlaws—The Next Generation*. Together with artist Joey Hartman-Dow, he has created the illustrated story, *The Amazing Adventures of the Afterbirth of Jesus*. A self-described Quirky, Queer, Quaker, Peterson speaks at universities, conferences, and in the media. As the host of Citizens' Climate Radio and the curator of ClimateStew.com, he draws on storytelling and comedy to present climate change as a human rights issues. His climate change presentations reveal the interconnectedness of power, privilege, justice, polar bears, and coffee beans. These include his performance lectures, *Everything is Connected—An evening of stories, most weird, many true and Climate Change—What's Faith Got to Do, Got to Do with It?* He lives in Central Pennsylvania with his partner, Glen Retief. www.petersontoscano.com

Made in the USA
Las Vegas, NV
25 January 2023